Maeve

Radiate Confidence

A Practical Guide Helping You to Build Confidence, Raise Your Self-Worth & Create the Life You Deserve

---

by Sharon Ledwith

Shine your light bright! ♡

Blessings & Love

Sharon Ledwith ♡

Copyright © 2019 Sharon Ledwith. All rights reserved.

This is a non-fiction book, and isn't meant to be a substitute for a doctor's or psychiatric help.

No parts of this book may be reproduced, distributed, or transmitted in any form without permission of the publisher.

Photocopying, recording, digital scanning, or other mechanic or electronic methods are not allowed, without the previous permission of the author.

ISBN: 9781689526753

First printing September 2019

Cover design by Maya Noonan

Dedication

This book is dedicated to my brother, Colin.

"No person is ever truly alone. Those who live no more, whom we loved, echo still within our thoughts, our words, our hearts. And what they did and who they were becomes a part of all we are, forever."

—Richard Fife

Contents

FOREWORD.. 1

AUTHOR FOREWORD 3

ACKNOWLEDGEMENTS 5

INTRODUCTION: SELF-CONFIDENCE AWARENESS – UNDERSTAND SELF-CONFIDENCE... 9

CHAPTER 1: SETTING AND ACHIEVING WORTHY GOALS 13

CHAPTER 2: THE IMPORTANCE OF ACCEPTANCE....................... 33

CHAPTER 3: MINDFULNESS.. 55

CHAPTER 4: CHANGING OLD BELIEFS 77

CHAPTER 5: THE LAW OF ATTRACTION 99

CHAPTER 6: MEDITATION 121

CHAPTER 7: MEDITATION FOR CONFIDENCE, ACCEPTANCE, AND CHANGE OF CORE BELIEFS 127

CHAPTER 8: AFFIRMATIONS 133

CONCLUSION 139

Foreword

S haron and I met a few years ago, and we instantly hit it off, as you do with someone who is on the same frequency or vibration as you are. Since then, I have seen Sharon really skyrocket forward by helping so many people!

Sharon and I are both go-getters by nature, and we both want to change lives, though our chosen fields are slightly different, with Sharon a wellness coach and myself a tech company founder.

I was so inspired by Sharon's attitude and confidence in life.

I came to learn that she hadn't always had such a positive and bold outlook, and what really touched and inspired me more than anything was discovering Sharon's story — her struggles in finding her why and her purpose!

It amazed me how focused and clear she was on her life purpose, and I have come to see true magnificence in her God-given gift of helping people the way she does.

In this book, you'll see for yourself the knowledge and understanding that Sharon has when it comes to helping you Radiate Confidence.

Sharon knows what it is like to struggle with a lack of self-belief and confidence, and through years of study and life experience, she is one of the best wellness coaches and energy healers I know. She is genuine and only has your best interests at heart, and her main objective with this book is to arm you with knowledge and to hopefully open up your self-awareness to really look deep within by taking on her guidance and teaching.

I am truly excited that you have purchased this book and are going to embark on this beautiful journey with her, opening a door to a new world of opportunities, one where you truly do *Radiate Confidence*!

With love and gratitude

Jackie Carroll
Tech Founder, Published Author & Speaker

Author Foreword

Sometimes we are not entirely aware of people, situations, and things that appear in our life. We might not like them at the beginning but, as time goes by and we learn more about them, we realize that they showed up to teach us something.

Dandelions are often seen as weeds — yellow flaws that ruin plush, green lawns. You see them everywhere, and maybe you haven't given a thought to these gentle and powerful plants.

Did you know that dandelions can grow anywhere and don't require special care? These strong plants appear in the early spring to remind us that the harsh winter is gone. When a dandelion turns into a tiny feathery universe, it needs only one blow to spread its little seed heads far away. The seed heads float gently in the air for hours till they reach the soil where they will grow.

The dandelion is the symbol for healing emotional pain, but also for intelligence in the spiritual and psychological meaning of the word. It symbolizes surviving challenges, as well as finding happiness, the fulfilment of wishes, and joy.

I like to think of my book as a dandelion. I am wholeheartedly spreading the little seeds to float to you. It is full of vibrant emotions, but also spiritual intelligence that I want to share with my readers. My intention is to help you grow, overcome your challenges, and learn more about yourself. In this book, you'll realize that you can be as gentle as a small dandelion, and still survive the harshest of times.

I wrote what I know best — and I encourage you to grow, heal, become aware of your thoughts, and keep your head up as you radiate confidence.

Blessings,

Sharon Ledwith

Acknowledgements

I want to thank my husband, Johnny, and my beautiful girls, Kellie and Eve. I also thank my Mam, Dad, and my sisters, Christine and Elaine, for their unconditional love, support, and belief in me in the past three years.

I am grateful to my friends and my clients for being there for me, loving me and accepting me for who I am. Thank you to Maya Noonan Photography for my pictures, a truly beautiful lady.

Finally, I want to thank you, dear reader, for giving my book a read. I hope you learn new things and go live your best life yet while radiating with confidence.

INTRODUCTION

Self-Confidence Awareness – Understand Self-Confidence

The media is overflowing with stories about confident people, how they do things, what they do differently from people who lack confidence, and they offer quick "lessons" that should help you become confident.

If there are so many pieces of advice available, then why are so many people lacking confidence and feeling insecure about themselves?

Let's go back to your early childhood. I bet you did not bother with thoughts of whether you looked good, if your clothes were cool, or whether you were saying the right things.

That's because children are not burdened with feeling this way. At what moment do we become so self-aware and sensitive about who we are, what we do, and our choices?

Society has a magical way of making us feel less worthy or even stupid. Why? Because it is our human nature to compare ourselves with others.

And you know what? This is a never-ending cycle that will drain your energy, ruin your self-respect and self-confidence, and leave you thinking that you are not good enough.

You are good enough!

We live in a world where comparisons are unavoidable. It happens at school, with your parents, your friends, your social groups, and perhaps even your partners do it.

The main question is, what can you do to become confident — truly confident, not just putting on a show in front of other people?

What does it mean to be genuinely and honestly confident?

It means to love yourself and respect who you are — as well as your choices, the way you look, the way you speak, your favourite things, your job, family, and home.

To be confident means that you are at peace and happy with the way you feel. There will always be someone better looking, smarter, and funnier than you, and that is entirely all right.

Confident people are not afraid to stand up for themselves. Lack of confidence will make you silent, wrapped in the opinion that you don't like conflicts, and you should remain silent. Confidence means that you're not afraid to say 'no' to people. It means that you are brave enough to tell people if something they do bothers you.

Being confident seems like another phrase, but it's possible. There was a time when I was not able to believe that I could ever be confident, happy, or live my best life.

It took me a long time to understand that confidence is like a muscle. The more you exercise, the more you strengthen your muscles, your posture, and improve your health — the healthier and stronger your body becomes.

The more you practice confidence, the stronger it becomes.

I am writing this book because I want to share the message with as many people as possible that we all have confidence. It isn't something you lack. It is something you need to awaken and grow it

INTRODUCTION: SELF-CONFIDENCE AWARENESS –
UNDERSTAND SELF-CONFIDENCE

enough to radiate, even if you've encountered challenging situations in your life.

You might think it is easy for the author to talk about confidence when she has always been this way. But you would be wrong.

Before we go any further, I want to share that the person writing these lines had two attempts of suicide. I did not always look or feel like this, and no matter what society now teaches us, my weight made me feel insecure and vulnerable. Depression was a normal state for me. I faced one of the biggest tragedies in life when my brother passed away through suicide.

I did not believe that life could ever be great for me. I was not able to see what my mission was, nor did I think that an abundant, calm, and pleasant life was ever in the cards for me.

After my second suicide attempt, something changed in me. I don't know what it was. Maybe my mind was tired, or my soul was fed up with feeling either sad or numb. Perhaps, my survival instinct kicked in. Sometimes, the universe has crazy plans for us. I came across a book that changed my life and felt as if I had finally opened my eyes. Maybe, I could change. One day I asked myself, Sharon if you had all the confidence in the world, what would you do?

The answers I came up with surprised me, and sort of liberated me. I asked myself, *"What stops me from doing all of this?"* Nothing. Just my old and stale beliefs that don't serve me any longer.

And it all started from there.

My main goal is to help you, dear reader, understand that you, too, have the power. Your thoughts are under your control. Your mind is a powerful tool, and your thoughts are just a stream that flows continuously. You are in charge of what thought will get your attention.

It took me a long time to understand this even though I read plenty of books, I meditated, connected with the angels, and did my best to upgrade my knowledge. But, now that I know certain things, I am happy and glad to share it with you.

I hope you'll give yourself time to read the following chapters and understand that you are capable of turning your life upside down, let go of every negative person and situation that does not serve you, get the pay rise you deserve, quit the job you hate, start working on something that fills your heart with joy and forgive yourself for everything.

CHAPTER 1

Setting and Achieving Worthy Goals

L et me start this chapter with a personal story, to which I am sure some of you can relate.

For a very long time, perhaps the more significant part of my life, I did not believe in myself. I always thought that I was not good enough. I am dyslexic, just like hundreds of thousands of people in the world. But, when I was young, I did not know there was a name for it, I just thought I was slower than others. I was so ashamed of my inability to read or write correctly, and I was always ashamed of my signature. I believed (and by this, I mean firmly) that I was not smart enough to learn new things, even though I worked hard at school because I believed I had to. I lived in fear that I would never be able to find a good job because I was stupid, inadequate, and slow.

Add to that mix that my weight was always at the higher end of the scales. Fortunately, I was not bullied. I was always good at talking to people, so children at school were not mean to me. But I was different, and when you're a child, it's a tragic thing to feel like you don't fit in.

I knew I was not stupid, but at the same time, my inner critic wouldn't shut up.

During my later teenage years, I lost weight and was finally able to look at myself in the mirror and like my physical appearance. Those years were not bad, but they brought other problems such as late nights out, alcohol use, and unhealthy relationships — anything to stop me from examining myself and my issues. My depression planted its seed in me, and although I was not fully aware of it then, it affected my relationship not only with myself but with other people as well.

Then, without warning, my brother passed through suicide. You can imagine what kind of shock it could be for a family. I was twenty-one years old, and when I remember those years, I see myself as a lost child, not a young adult. I was living away from home, crying a lot, finding it hard to cope with all that was going on and still trying to get through each day.

The years that followed were not pleasant at all. I lived for another couple of years wholly devastated, sad, and entirely drowned in a deep depression. I was vibrating so low that I naturally attracted negative people and situations in my life. My life was a circle of negativity in which I was lost and did not know how to change it. During those years was when I tried to end my life twice.

By the time I turned 24, fed up with it all, I had moved to Australia. I met my now-husband, and things seemed to move up from ground zero.

Life started happening. I got a job, but it was doing something for which I was over-qualified. But, when you lack confidence and are not able to appreciate your capabilities and self-worth, and that your purpose is much higher than working a job you don't like, you can end up having a job you dislike for years because you feel stuck.

I wanted to quit my job and do something else. It was not because I felt I was better than anyone else, but that there was no growth there for me. You see, when you have two children, and you work the morning shift, you realize that you are missing the most precious moment of your children's childhood. My biggest wish was to spend more time at home with my children. But, because of my fear and not having enough money, confidence, and self-worth, I stayed at my job. I wasn't brave enough to get out of my comfort zone and seek a more challenging position.

CHAPTER 1 — SETTING AND ACHIEVING WORTHY GOALS

I didn't do it until I realized that my self-sabotage had nothing to do with my qualities, education, skills, or work experience. It had to do with my repetitive behaviour, depression, fear of life, and limiting beliefs.

When I had my second child, my vibration hit a low again, and I felt that deep sadness trying to sneak back in. Now I can see it was a blessing in disguise, as this was a time when I started my spiritual journey. I embarked upon my natural journey. I developed an interest in reading books that were real eye-openers. In doing so, I discovered *The Secret* by Rhonda Byrne, plus Bob Proctor, Reiki, and the angels.

Reading books on and watching programmes about spiritualism, higher self, depression, thoughts, and emotions helped me realize a few things. I learned about limiting beliefs and immediately recognized that I was doing a lot of stuff restraining my full potential, believing I was not good enough or smart enough.

We all have beliefs about various things, and I don't mean religiously.

People believe in many things. They think they're not good looking, not good enough, and maybe dependent on a partner because they're not strong enough to do things on their own. Some of us believe that we are unloveable or that we don't deserve such love in our lives. I know this can be a real challenge.

These beliefs may have been instilled by ourselves, or by another person or situation, such as a friend, parent, teacher, or conditionings.

What is good and bad about our beliefs is that no matter what you believe about yourself, you're usually right.

So how is it possible to believe that you're not good enough, and be right about it?

When you've firmly convinced yourself about some belief, you create your life around it. Let's say you believe you can't climb a tree because you haven't done that in years. You think that you cannot lift yourself and climb a few branches because you're no longer a child. You believe that if you try to climb that tree, you might fall or even break your leg.

So, you don't climb the tree: your belief remains firm. You're not going to do it today, nor tomorrow. You say you cannot climb trees, period. But, if you try to do it and succeed, you realize that you were convincing yourself about something entirely wrong. You are capable of climbing a tree without hurting yourself. None of the invented stories in your head (broken leg) came true.

Your limiting beliefs only serve you to live a life that isn't satisfying. It makes you think that something is this way when, in reality, it is something completely different.

Not everybody is lucky or awakened enough to realize this simple fact, so some people go through their entire lives living their limiting beliefs — a sure way to live the same experience, every day until the day they die. It means to believe that nothing can change, that you are this way or that way, only bad things happen to you, etc.

I know that many people are afraid of change, but nothing is more constant than change. And it happens, whether we want it to happen or not. The main question is, are we are capable of understanding our limiting beliefs so we can start shedding them like old skin?

What Are Limiting Beliefs?

Not everyone learns that their lives are the way they are because of their limiting beliefs. Some people never get the chance to learn what a limiting belief is.

To change your limiting belief, you must first identify it. Just like when identifying a disease, you have to get diagnosed and then take action to get better.

I don't say it is a piece of cake to identify your limiting beliefs. Some of us believe that most of the old beliefs are our traits ("that's just the way it is," or "get on with it," for instance).

I had many limiting beliefs. And it was challenging for me to identify, acknowledge, and start working on breaking them!

Sometimes, you need to realize that some things in your life don't go smoothly because you create issues in your head, and then you begin to believe in them.

CHAPTER 1 – SETTING AND ACHIEVING WORTHY GOALS

I don't want to blame you, your parents, friends, teachers. People don't make you believe in something by force. Usually, when limiting beliefs are instilled in us by our family, it is because our parents and siblings also had limiting beliefs. They, too, were taught to believe things like life is hard; money does not grow on trees; nothing comes easily; marriage is tough, and so on.

It is a generational problem, but we are here to identify it and start healing ourselves and our children.

Here is how I identified all of my limiting beliefs.

I took a piece of paper and drew a line down the middle.

On the left, I wrote all my limiting beliefs. On the right, I wrote beliefs that would serve me better.

Limiting Beliefs That Don't Serve Me	Beliefs That Serve Me Well
People find it hard to love me. I am not good enough. I am boring. Life will never change. Money is bad. People are dishonest. I look terrible and it's something that will never change. My dyslexia stops me from success.	I love myself. I take care of me. I eat well. I go places that make me happy. Slowly, but surely, I am dropping my limiting beliefs, because it feels good to have good thoughts. What other people think of me has nothing to do with me. In fact, they don't even think that much of me. Which is great. I am changing my life every day. Every positive thought helps me raise my vibration. I work at what I love and earn money easily.

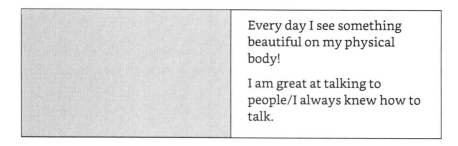

Every day I see something beautiful on my physical body!

I am great at talking to people/I always knew how to talk.

And did this list help? Absolutely!

I would be lying if I said that it worked immediately. Limiting beliefs have deep roots, and when you read or write positive thoughts, your mind screams, "Lie!"

So I found another way to trick my mind.

I read my list of limiting beliefs (it was far longer than this one) out loud and asked myself, Sharon, would you say this crap to your five-year-old self? Would you say these things to your adolescent self?

Tears came to my eyes immediately, and I knew that I was on the right track.

Why would you feed yourself with negativity that doesn't serve you? It doesn't matter how old you are or what you do. You are a child at heart. Why would you poison yourself with such thoughts every day? Why would you believe such things?

Changing your limiting beliefs won't take place overnight.

Some will go away quickly, while others will require more effort.

The stubborn ones will tell you which area in your life needs healing. It is your job to get to the original hurt.

Perhaps you were taught that you should be content with what you have (which isn't necessarily a bad thing). The problem occurs when you're told you that you shouldn't fantasize about jobs that are not meant for you, and with time, you start to believe these things. You see rich people as dishonest and think they got their money by doing something illegal, or that "money follows money."

So how can that limiting belief affect your goals?

CHAPTER 1 – SETTING AND ACHIEVING WORTHY GOALS

In my case, it was tightly connected.

My limiting beliefs stopped me from finding a better job (that gave me growth) for years. I am sure it fed my depression, too.

I lived a life with no challenges, goals, or intentions. Although I have an excellent partner and two beautiful girls, I was numb from feeling "less than." I was filled with negative thoughts about myself, and deep sadness was setting in. I honestly could not see where I was going.

Going through the day seemed like a dream. Every day was the same as the one before, and there was nothing that could excite me.

So how did change happen?

As I said in the introduction, I was not a happy person on the inside. I even tried to end my life twice. I did not know how to change how I felt, how to make bad feelings go away, or how to change my thoughts. People judge depressed, suicidal people, all while we carry a heavy weight. We don't feel like dying, and we don't want to leave our families; we want peace from the mind.

My first goal (even before I knew that goals and confidence are connected) was to lose weight. I was in my earlier years when my will to change how I looked was stronger than anything else.

I established a goal to walk twice a day for twenty minutes and limit my food intake to three meals a day. I gave myself a reasonable deadline of four months, yet I endured for a full four months and more. And I had visible results that made me feel good.

I felt more confident. I was not able to detect that feeling back then — all I knew was that I felt great.

But my eye-opening moment happened when I discovered The Secret and Bob Proctor videos. Before then, I didn't pay attention to things like visualization, setting goals, the power of our mind, or spiritualism. But the information I read made me hungry for more knowledge and, of course, for proof that what I was reading was real.

My next goal, while I was working on my spiritualism and education, was to leave my job. I was not happy there, but what was eating me on the inside was the feeling of guilt that I didn't spend enough time with my children.

Once I set the goal, I took action. I read everything related to my new topics of interest. On the weekends, I took courses. My knowledge and interests widened so much that I could not get enough learning about meditation, Reiki, psychic development, healing, angels, etc.

I wanted to keep improving myself, which was my other goal — to become more educated and to enrich my knowledge as much as I could.

I visualized my current job. Since I was always a great speaker, talking to people came easily for me. My first focus shift helped me to raise my vibration. I no longer felt sad because I was not the best with grammar and spelling. Instead, I focused on the knowledge that my talent for speaking would be of great use for me.

I am not writing these lines to brag.

To set a goal means to have something that will move you forward. It does not have to be a huge thing. Sometimes big goals scare us, especially if we are vulnerable and in a healing phase.

You can start by setting your intention for the day. It can be as "insignificant" as avoiding food that doesn't benefit your body. It can be to set a doctor's appointment you've been avoiding. It can be a bigger goal, such as finding a new job, writing a book, finishing college, or working on your subjects at school. Trust me, the moment you set your intention, something will change in you. The universe will make a shift, and you'll feel it, and you'll know it.

The moment you achieve your goal is the moment when your confidence starts to radiate outward. The busier you are with achieving your goals, the more your confidence will grow. People will start noticing the shift in you.

Start acknowledging your effort once you achieve your goal. It doesn't have to be something big. Did you finish your entire work within a day? Have a coffee in the park before going home. Have you graduated after long and challenging years? Allow yourself to rest

CHAPTER 1 – SETTING AND ACHIEVING WORTHY GOALS

without feeling guilty. Look at yourself in the mirror and thank yourself out loud for your accomplishment.

We often forget to thank ourselves for our achievements. Sometimes success can be as "little" as getting out of bed. It could be walking to work, helping someone else, or getting a significant promotion.

You accomplish these things every day. I ask you to understand that your effort is essential. You matter — as a person. The things you did today matter. So, give yourself credit and reward yourself with small things. Allow your soul to feel good. You must get used to feeling good, and nothing feels better than when you're aware that you're capable of doing things. Give yourself that self-recognition you deserve.

Achieving your goals is perhaps one of the first steps that will improve your self-confidence. Maybe you believe that it's easy for me to say it now that I have passed through my bad times. But I continue to work on myself every day. I know that my growth never stops, and we should never stop learning and moving forward.

Here is the thing that helped me.

It is important to trick your mind. You might wonder how that's possible when it seems like lying to yourself.

But your mind does not know what's real. You are continually overthinking and worry over things and situations that have about a 5 percent chance of happening. You are accustomed to creating a fake reality for your mind. You suffer and feel sick, anxious, scared, and destructive.

How about trying a little experiment and start thinking of things that work out for you? Focus on thoughts that make you feel good. Visualize the things you want to achieve. Dedicate about one or two minutes of your day to visualize yourself achieving the goal you have set.

Remember, you shouldn't think about how you'll do it, or when. Just see yourself buying that car, getting a promotion, getting accepted in your preferred college, getting that new job. And then let it go. Forget about it. Continue doing your thing.

What is crucial is to allow this visualization to create a good feeling.

It was challenging for me to do this until I let myself go. I visualized myself working with people, talking to them, sharing my story and everything I knew with them. My vision was so strong that I was able to visualize every little detail about the holistic business I have today.

I did not worry whether it would become real or not. I loved how my visualizations were making me feel, and that was the most important thing. Once I visualized my goal, I let it go and continued with my actions.

And then, miracles started happening.

I know that the word miracle is often overused. For many people, the word miracle is just that, a word, something that happens in fairy tales, not in your everyday life.

Let's be realistic: we are all miracles. You were born, you are here now, you have organs that work together to keep you alive. Your body knows how to heal itself (every day, your cells are fighting bad cells, preventing them from turning into a deadly disease). We live on a planet that floats in a vast dark space, surrounded by other planets and a massive sun that gives us light and warmth.

We take this for granted, but just one change in the solar system can make all of this beauty on our planet go away.

The moment you start seeing the miracles, the moment when you voluntarily decide to observe the world around you like a place with possibilities, you'll begin to witness beautiful things.

Setting a goal isn't only a test to see whether you can achieve it or not. Chances are, you'll complete it successfully. The main reason why setting a goal is one of the most recommended activities to build your confidence, is because it gives you purpose.

All of a sudden, you have something on which to focus. Your thoughts are not wandering, and your mind isn't attached to the wrong things.

You think of ways to achieve this goal you set for yourself.

CHAPTER 1 – SETTING AND ACHIEVING WORTHY GOALS

Lack of activity means trapping your energy. You let it become stale. You sit and observe everyone else working, trying harder, achieving things, going places. Your mind forces you to compare yourself with them.

This person traveled around Europe, and I am doing nothing.

This person just landed the job of my dreams, and I am stuck in the old post that I hate.

This person just lost extra weight, and I am unable to fit in the jeans I bought a few months ago.

Such thoughts are a recipe for disaster. Nothing will work out if you sit and compare yourself to others. It is like letting mice nibble on your confidence until it is completely gone (or at least peppered with millions of little holes.)

The moment you decide to set and achieve a goal, you move on from the dead point. You take steps forward — you are doing something for yourself. It does not have to be a huge thing, nor should you compare your activities or goals with the goals of others.

It is essential that you are moving forward and that there is something that gives you fuel. Once you have started the engine, your activities (that will help you achieve the goal) are leading you in the direction you want to go.

Suddenly, you don't have time to think about what another person has achieved. Now you are too busy working on your goal.

How to Set a Goal

Some people don't think they need to set goals once their life is settled. They believe that living in a routine (get up, have coffee, go to work, come home, eat dinner, sleep) isn't a bad thing. They achieved something — finished college, got a job, had a family — and that is more than enough.

Maybe for some people, this isn't enough at all.

If you are awakening and feel that something has to change, especially when it comes to your confidence, you have to set a goal, which might seem like an easy task, but for some people, it's a real challenge.

Society, school, parents, teachers and even the programmes we watch on TV can make us forget what we want.

More often than not, people are doing things they believe they like to do, when in fact these desires have been instilled in them by other people. You see thousands of people spending money on expensive phones or cars, just because the ad convinced them that they needed these items. Other people do things because they see others do them.

They end up being unhappy, stressed, and lack confidence because they are doing things they don't enjoy. They are doing things dishonestly, only to look good in front of others.

I decided to change my life by setting a goal. It was the beginning of a fantastic change. And what's more important is that I wanted this change. I needed to become the real me. My numbness slowly started dissipating.

Once you set your goal, don't stop. The only thing that drives you forward is your urge and need to see yourself doing something you set your intention on. In my case, I continually built a picture of helping hundreds of people change and release their old self-limiting beliefs. I visualized doing all of this in my holistic centre.

If you think that this is just some New Age crap, let me tell you that 12 months after I set my goal, I handed in my notice at my old work, and three weeks later I opened my own business.

It's been three years, and I'm still running a successful holistic business. My vision was to talk to people and help them release their old beliefs and unlock their potential. I spend more time at home, and I bring my children to and from school. My husband, as well, decided to change shifts (he no longer works in the evenings) and we spend our evenings together.

I encourage you to take a pen and paper and write a list of things that you enjoy doing.

Perhaps you love sports, but you don't have the time to play. Maybe you used to dance in the past but then stopped as life got too busy.

CHAPTER 1 – SETTING AND ACHIEVING WORTHY GOALS

Write a list of the goals that you would like to achieve. If you want, write in detail how you would feel if you reached specific goals. Do not give your mind the chance to trick you into thinking that this is mission impossible. Do not hang onto thoughts that are screaming, *"Don't set a goal that cannot be achieved! You'll be disappointed!"*

It was a struggle for me, but I managed to fight my thoughts when I wrote down that I wanted to become a spiritual life coach. I wrote down that I wanted to help people awaken and see their potential, and I wanted to be there for them on their journey.

I became quite vocal about my goals. In the beginning, I was a bit shy, but as my vibration changed and I started achieving my smaller goals, I felt that I was no longer in the same place I used to be and confidently started expressing all my goals to others.

New people started appearing in my life. Sometimes talking to a stranger feels sweeter than talking to a person you know for a long time. Life offers you people who are good for you at the right moment. I am grateful for those people who showed interest in talking to me. Lack of confidence can make you feel as if nobody cares when you genuinely want someone to care. The truth is, you need to care first — you need to care about yourself.

I don't know what sort of people surround you. Sometimes it can be tricky to tell your parents, siblings, partner, or friends about your plans.

If you are still hesitant to speak of the things that you are interested in (your goals and focus), then you don't have to do it. The main thing is to stay focused and never quit working towards making your goal your reality.

Some people find it easier to go through their journey when they verbalize the goal — it motivates them. When you say things out loud, you become more aware of them. It seems like they are real.

Remember, your goal does not have to be a thing that will change the world. Your goal can be something that does not even affect other people.

Perhaps you want to read every day for one hour. Maybe your goal is to become a vegan. You want to set a goal to work out in the gym three days a week. Or you want to save a certain amount of money by the end of the year.

To set a goal might be complicated at first, but once you place it, the trickier part comes: you make your goals a priority.

It was easy to write down what you want to achieve, but can you find the time and the will to work on these goals? Can you fight your procrastination?

Some people work best with timelines and deadlines. For me, setting deadlines (for my weight loss and writing this book) works well. I felt that I should give myself a reasonable amount of time during which I would work until I reached my goals.

Even after I started working on my spiritual journey, I continued to set goals that would thrill me enough so that I would not fall victim to procrastination.

I started with small steps. I didn't force myself to do anything that would make me feel anxious. My only concern while I was working on my goals was to feel good. If achieving my goals didn't feel like a burden or obligation, then it couldn't be a bad thing.

I managed to rewire my brain successfully into thinking that setting and achieving a goal brings me happiness, and that helped me feel better about myself. It helped me improve my fragile confidence and stand taller.

You know, it does feel nice when you can say, "I did this."

Not because others will pat your shoulders, but because you'll feel better about yourself. An achieved goal releases chemicals in your brain and makes you feel proud. Once you get a taste of this feeling, you would not want to feel any other way.

The more goals you set, the better your chances are of accomplishing them.

I'm not recommending that you start by setting ten goals and then get lost in the process. Set one primary goal that will hold your focus.

CHAPTER 1 — SETTING AND ACHIEVING WORTHY GOALS

Then, place a few other (secondary) goals that will help you achieve the primary one.

You know what's best is for you. You can easily determine how big of a goal you can accomplish.

I pointed out that my first goal was to lose weight even before I knew about goals, and before I became spiritual.

Your goal should work to improve you as a person — emotionally, physically, and mentally. You should feel excited and happy while you are working on the process. Your goal should be the fuel that helps you move forward. Finally, your goal should help you set other goals that would help you work on the big picture you want to create for yourself.

But, there is a challenge in setting goals. There are millions of people who set goals and don't achieve them. Sure, it isn't the end of the world, but if you want to do this the right way, let me give you a few helpful tips.

Many people set a goal to become rich and that's it. Their only goal is to have money. They don't put any detail into the goal. Some people achieve a goal they had no desire for, but they did it anyway because it was somebody else's idea, or they thought the goal would make someone else happier.

In the first case, when a person lacks a clear and detailed vision, his or her goal will easily be lost somewhere in the process. When your concept is vague, and you don't know precisely why you want this goal, you can end up procrastinating. Doing something else will become much more interesting for you than working to achieve your goal.

I always tell the people I work with that they must be very detailed about the goal. By details, I don't mean to overthink how you'll work on it or when it will manifest. By detailed vision, see yourself achieving this goal. If your goal is getting a new car, see yourself sitting behind the wheel, driving down the road. Visualize the interior, the colour of your new ride. Visualize the sides of the road — green grass, beautiful houses, a straight and smooth road. See your hands on the wheel, feel the comfort of the seat. See how your hand moves towards the radio, seeking a song that makes you feel great. Sing this song while you are driving your new car.

That is a detailed vision. Don't think when you'll buy this car, nor where you'll find it. That is none of your concern. The biggest goal of your vision is to feel great while visualizing. And when you feel great, you raise your vibration. The higher you vibrate, the closer you are to the things you want. Everything you want is already yours. You have to feel great while working on the process. And never stop believing that this thing will come to you.

In the second case, when people set goals because someone else wanted them to achieve them, they usually succeed. People end up studying in a college their mother thought was the best for them. Or, you see people doing a job because their parents believed it was the best choice for them. The main question is, are they happy?

Usually, the answer is no. They have accomplished someone else's dream and goal. They did it, and they can be proud of their work and effort, but there is nothing more exhausting and unfulfilling than doing an unfulfilling thing.

It is like eating 'bland' food; it's something that keeps you alive but has no taste. Such things might seem insignificant. But when people allow other people to control their life, make choices for them, or even instill their wishes as to the best option, it's a sure way to create unhappy people. You will wonder why you cannot be happy with your accomplished goal when everyone says that you ought to feel great once you achieve it. There is something that stops you from feeling great, and you cannot detect it.

When you work on your goal and finally start to see the desired results, you'll feel how your confidence grows stronger. You will no longer walk around with your head buried in your chest. People will start noticing that good things are happening for you, and you'll be confident enough to smile and affirm that it is true.

Set a goal that will thrill you. Set a goal that will scare you. It is crucial that you feel good about working toward your goal. Sometimes, there will be struggles. Other times, you'll make it without any obstacles.

CHAPTER 1 – SETTING AND ACHIEVING WORTHY GOALS

The key lies in your determination, will, and the quality of your thoughts.

We will discuss these things in the following chapters, but I want to instill it in your mind that working on a goal in your life will make you feel great.

When you achieve something (because you wanted it, not because your friends or parents thought it was a good idea), your brain gets the info that you have done something right and releases chemicals that make you feel happy, confident, and content.

To achieve your goal, it does not take hard work, but smart work. I don't say you should find the easiest ways, but to find the methods that work best for you.

And start learning. I don't care what degrees you have, what schools you went to, there is no such thing as too much learning. Find literature that is related to your goal. Read it and then read some more. Become thirsty for knowledge. Let yourself see this process of achieving your goal as another way to improve yourself.

If your goal is to save money by the end of the month, start reading online financial blogs. Read economy books. Start watching videos or attend master classes with people who know about these things. Maybe you'll awaken an interest you never knew you had, and the next thing you know, your goal can take you to a whole new different life path. You might end up finding a new job, starting your own business, or investing in your knowledge.

The crucial thing for a successful goal accomplishment is to know whether your values connect with what you want to achieve. You should know your values. If for example, you are a curious person who loves learning new things, your goal will have to resonate with this value of yours. So, if your goal is finding a job, then landing any job will mean that you have accomplished it. But if your job does not satisfy your curiosity and numbs you day by day, have you succeeded?

I always ask people to be completely honest about their passion: then their genuine picture of becoming who they always wanted to be can happen much easier and faster.

Whatever your goal is, it should make you happy. You are the one who is trying to achieve these things, not your parents, your followers on social media, or your neighbours.

To achieve a goal means that you'll have to do things you did not do before. If you want to save money, you'll have to stop recklessly spending. If you're going to achieve better results in your weight loss process, you'll have to stop eating as much and exercising more.

Whatever your goal is, it will (in most cases) require you to change some old habits, or at least learn new ones.

A goal should inspire you to do something different that would change you and improve you as a person. Every achieved goal sends information to your brain, and your brain releases happy hormones.

Once your brain gets used to these feelings, it will give its best to "make you" work more on such things.

Confident and successful people are always busy working on something. They are addicted to this feeling, and who can blame them?

I want you to understand that confidence isn't something that can be built overnight. See it as building a house. You have to start from the basics, then slowly progress towards building the first floor, second floor (make as many levels as you want). Finally, you get to work on the rooftop.

See this process as building your muscles, as I mentioned at the beginning. You don't get to see your biceps grow huge after one week at the gym. You will need plenty of time to achieve that, but time shouldn't set you back, because time will pass anyway.

Let your desire for improvement, for building your muscles (your confidence) guide you. The progress will become visible sooner or later, so it shouldn't worry you. But remember that the only person you are allowed to compare yourself with is the person you used to be.

You cannot compare your muscles to that bodybuilder in the gym. God knows how long he or she was working on their body. You don't

CHAPTER 1 – SETTING AND ACHIEVING WORTHY GOALS

know how challenging it was for them, so it would be a real shame to compare yourself with them.

You can see them as an inspiration, but never as competition.

The same goes with confidence. A confident person might have been through thick and thin. Only they know how long they worked to achieve their goals and how long it took them to feel good in their skin, without the need to compare themselves to others.

Sometimes it can be as easy as putting beautiful clothes on. Other times it would take a great accomplishment.

This is why I dedicated my first chapters to goals. Once you give yourself the freedom to set a goal and decide that you no longer want to feel this way, you have made the shift.

Now it's time for you to believe in the universe a little more. It's time to believe in yourself a little more. It's time for you to start thinking that you can do this. Even if you fail, you'll be alright. You tried, and you dedicated yourself to this goal. You failed, but you stood up — that is what this is all about.

The moment you realize that achieving your goals isn't a competition is the moment when you feel the freedom you need to succeed. Achieving your goals that will boost your confidence has nothing to do with other people.

You are reading these lines because you want to feel better, improve, and become better than you were yesterday. Your goal is to achieve the things you believe you can already do, but you need a little support.

I don't have to tell you when the right time is for you to start the change. By deciding to read a book of this category, you have already decided on the timing. Now, you are taking action. You are reading content that will help you awaken and realize what you knew from the beginning, but somehow you were forced to forget. You deserve the life that would make you feel you are happy to wake up. Live a life that would not feel like a burden.

You are here because your main goal is to accept who you truly are. And I will gladly help you in the process of building your confidence and accepting who you are in your full divinity.

CHAPTER 2

The Importance of Acceptance

People continuously speak about acceptance — self-acceptance, acceptance of others, acceptance of the situation you are in, etc.

Look around yourself. Notice the people who are your friends, family, co-workers, and neighbours. Notice even strangers you see in the streets and parks.

If you pay enough attention, you'll see people who don't show significant signs of self-acceptance. The main reason behind that is because their confidence might not be the strongest. But, to find the real reason for that, you'll perhaps have to dig a little deeper.

From our earliest days, most of us are taught to do this or that so we can blend in. Our parents tell us to quit misbehaving because girls should be seen and not heard. You have perhaps heard at least once, "Do you see other children misbehaving?" For the boys, it was the same. They are taught from their earliest days to be tough, that tears are for girls, pink is for girls, to pick a colour that is socially acceptable for boys. Behave the way boys should behave.

We are conditioned from the very beginning that we must do things that will be acceptable to others. No matter if these things are not working with our emotions, choices, and thoughts, we are convinced they are okay to please others.

This is the easiest way to condition people who have fragile self-confidence; those who feel they must do things so others will accept them, give them credit and a compliment — when on the inside they feel terrible.

Many people ask me what they can do to boost their confidence. Is there a magic wand to get rid of their inner feelings of not being good enough, or pretty or successful enough? Do I know a way that will help them feel calm and at peace with who they are?

There is no magic wand, nor can you change overnight. It takes time to unlearn what we have been taught for years, but if you are willing to work at it, then with support, it is possible to change.

As I mentioned already, our parents, society, teachers, friends, films, and television are continually instilling in us feelings and beliefs about money, health, love, success.

And sometimes, especially when you are in your vulnerable years, you learn things when other people's opinions are so important, and you accept these beliefs.

This is how we end up depressed, without enough self-love, and doing things that other people want us to do. We try to impress others to get a compliment, be praised, or feel accepted.

We are not here to blame others. It seems that the entire system (everyone on this planet) works that way. What makes me happy is the fact that I am seeing new parents and young people who are awake and more aware of the importance of self-acceptance and self-love.

How can we accept and love ourselves when social media offers a ton of filters and face changers that are supposed to be fun, but in the end they create a very unrealistic picture of who we are and how we look?

Social media, dating and beauty apps, phones — all of these are just "tools" that help us improve our "flaws."

You can't expect a teenage boy or girl to build a healthy acceptance of their appearance when they are under constant pressure to look a certain way. Young men and women are under so much stress due

CHAPTER 2 — THE IMPORTANCE OF ACCEPTANCE

to excessive use of social media that only leads to reduced confidence and mental health issues.

I understand that these things are not supposed to be taken seriously. When you log in to your social media application, you see that most women and men look the same. They accepted one generic look (that was somehow glorified and pushed down people's throats as the best and most appealing).

When I was struggling with my weight, society was much more into body shaming. Perhaps people were not going to say it to your face, but the mocking towards people who were not a size 0 was everywhere. It was a time when you rarely saw overweight people on film or in print. Magazines, papers, and TV had long been criticized for upholding dangerously unrealistic standards of success and beauty.

Today the standards are set much closer to home, not only by celebrities and models but by classmates and friends, peers, and colleagues. With social media, people can curate their lives, and the resulting feeds read like highlight reels, showing only the best and most enviable moments while concealing efforts, struggles and the ordinary aspects of day-to-day life.

For the longest time, I wasn't able to accept myself. You might wonder, "Why is the author writing about self-acceptance when she was continually trying to lose weight? That is the first sign of not accepting yourself."

There were many reasons why I was trying to lose weight. I wanted to have a healthier body and to look better. But it wasn't until recently that I realized that these attempts were nothing but my way of trying to do something that would make me happy.

We are always doing things we believe will make us happier because we feel that something isn't right. We will be happier or feel better when we buy that car. We believe that our confidence will reach the sky when we get promoted at work. Or perhaps our lives will fall in place when we get this person to love us or go to that place.

Sure, these things are confidence boosters, but will our inner feelings change?

Many people struggle to understand that the base of our happiness lies in us. You don't need any external stimulation, person, or thing to feel better once you decide to be happy. Once you choose to change your focus from the things you lack to the things you are already blessed with, a shift will take place.

For some, this happens easier and faster. For others, it may take some time and help.

I have talked to many people who believed they were confident and that they had accepted themselves. But after a few questions, they realized that they still had a lot of work to do.

When I discuss this subject, I often ask people whether they have become the person they always wanted to be. Usually, the first answer is yes, but with hesitation. They return to their childhood and think of all the ideas they had about themselves. Naturally, life happens in between, and we often make choices that are not so dreamy. This is when people become defensive, and I get answers such as, "I am waiting on redundancy to leave," or "Well you know, painting does not pay off," or "I'm too old to start college now," and so on.

This shows me that no matter how old you are or what you are working at, you still hold that initial picture of yourself — who you want to be and what you want to do.

Usually, I ask people to forget about their current situation and tell me in detail who they want to be.

Please do the same. Write down a short story and describe in detail who you want to be as a person.

Please, make sure you skip things such as "I want to be a rich person who owns ten cars, two houses, and a yacht." They may come along but isn't the focus of this writing exercise.

Perhaps you want to be a person who can easily say no to people. Maybe you want to be unbothered by other people's opinions. Maybe you want to make decisions without constantly worrying about whether parents or partners will accept your decisions.

CHAPTER 2 – THE IMPORTANCE OF ACCEPTANCE

Write the most honest and open idea of who you want to be as a person. Be as detailed as possible. Don't be afraid that some of the things you write down don't resonate with you now. This is your written vision of who you want to become.

Now, get another sheet and write down in detail the things that make you happy. It can be anything. Perhaps you love and enjoy having your coffee in silence, for instance. Write about the big and little things that make you feel happy.

Finally, end this little writing exercise by answering the following questions:

What holds me back?

Who holds me back?

How will my life change if I eventually let go of these things or people?

Be brutally honest. It can be challenging when it comes to people, but sometimes we have to let go of toxic relationships.

I don't say this lightly, as I know that many people deal with negativity from very close people such as family. People often ask me what to do in cases like this, and my answer is always the same — if you cannot cut the cords, then cut the time you spend with these people. Make sure you continue to work on yourself while letting go of the old to allow change to happen.

Now read your story out loud. How do you feel? Does this person you want to become resonate with you? Does it spark joy in you, or do you feel like it is too much, and that people would probably dislike you?

It isn't fair to blame others for our lack of confidence or our inability to accept ourselves, but sometimes, people and the things we do have a significant effect on how we feel and why we can or cannot move forward.

Of course, ending negative relations or quitting bad habits can be a challenge, but to make the first step towards accepting that you need an environment without bad energy and bad vibes means that you'll have to continue sailing on this journey without certain things and people.

Here is the thing in this exercise.

Some parents believe if they criticize their children, they will inspire them to make something more, to try harder, and so on. These people don't realize that they are doing more damage than good to their children. I intentionally give you this example with parents, because even the people who love you the most can do damage that can cost you years to unlearn and break old and stale beliefs.

I have two amazing daughters, and my main goal is to show them that I love them just the way they are. I accept their choices, guide them when they need to see the larger picture, protect them from possible hurts, and support them when they need it.

People who lacked acceptance and support from home will always try to substitute it in another form. They end up working their hardest to get recognition, applause, and a little admiration from people who might not mean anything in their life.

The best thing a parent can do for their child (or a partner for their partner, sibling for their sibling) is to make it clear that a person first needs to accept themselves in every meaning of the word.

The world is full of people who say negative things to people who are not like them. I always tell my children and my clients that when someone says something about you, it is a reflection of how they feel inside about themselves.

In the best cases, these people go through life living the way they want. But what happens with the thousands of people who are not brave enough to face their families and blindly accept the role their parents, family, and society gave them? The role they play is plausible, but are they happy?

How to Accept Yourself

I can write down a few sentences with motivational words and tell you to go and accept yourself. But will this work? No, it won't.

CHAPTER 2 – THE IMPORTANCE OF ACCEPTANCE

Accepting yourself, especially when you were told to do things that were acceptable by your parents, teachers, friends, and society, can be quite a challenge. You'll have to work on this day by day.

Don't let this set you back, as we all have our struggles, and we all go through things like this. Some days are great, and on other days you'll need some more effort.

Now that I asked you to write a short story on who you want to be as a person, what things you care about, and what things and people are no longer serving your journey, here comes the practical part.

I am not going to tell you to read this story every day. It does not work that way.

My suggestion is to start practising forms of self-acceptance.

What does it mean to do this?

First of all, let's make it clear what are the forms of self-acceptance.

One way is to stop complaining. And I mean to forbid yourself from talking about the challenges in your life — and, avoid using the word problem. Stop saying that things are not working out for you. Stop saying that you can't lose weight, or that you cannot get that pay rise, or that you cannot have a good relationship.

Did you know that negative self-talk is one of the main reasons why you continuously feel terrible? Every time you catch yourself saying negative things about yourself, STOP.

I always point out my example. I was not a person who was able to accept a compliment. Anytime someone said something nice to me, instead of thanking them, I said, "Thank you, but..." or "Stop, I look terrible today."

I did my best to tell them that their compliments were not realistic. I said things like, "Thank you, but this isn't a new dress, I've had it for years," "Thank you, but no, it's really not a big deal," "Thank you, but I didn't lose weight, you must be seeing things."

When I started raising my vibration and reading more about personal growth, affirmations, negative self-image, confidence, and self-acceptance, I realized that everything I was doing was ruining my attempts to improve my confidence.

The next time someone pays you a compliment, say thank you without any additional explaining. It may be hard if you have a hard time believing in the praise. Often people tell me that other people give compliments when they want something from you, meaning the compliment isn't their real opinion.

I always say it is none of your business whether they mean it or not. Your job is to give thanks and continue with your day. Compliments are nice and can make you feel good, but if you need to ruin the compliment with an explanation, then you don't agree with the words.

I often ask people whether it's better if the compliment is sincere, or if you agree with the kind words.

The answer is always the latter.

Why are we so prone to negative self-talk and complaining? Why are we so dedicated to telling others how we failed, how things are not well, etc.?

The answer is simple — we haven't accepted ourselves yet.

Have you heard a confident person complain? Even if things are not working for them at that moment, they don't worry. They try other options and see the failure as a lesson and are eager to try again.

A confident person won't spend two hours complaining or telling you that they look terrible, that their hair is a mess, or that they have a hard time learning a new thing. When you pay them a compliment, they smile and thank you, and then talk about something else.

Another form of self-acceptance is to see failure as a regular thing. Confident people don't see failure as the end of the world. Yes, sometimes it can be difficult, but it's essential to continue living, trying, and working. Lack of self-acceptance and confidence deliver sadness and make you think failure is your fault. You add even more burden to yourself in believing that you are not good enough, or destined to make it. You seek the blame in yourself and feed with even more negative self-talk. You are only restraining from challenges

CHAPTER 2 – THE IMPORTANCE OF ACCEPTANCE

out of fear of failure, believing that you are safe where you are. In absolutely every case, such behaviour leads towards negativity, not just towards yourself, but to others. It's no wonder people who can't accept themselves and lack confidence are so defensive and negative towards others.

My suggestion is to start writing down and saying out loud three things you love about yourself, both physically and mentally. Look at yourself in the mirror and start seeking the good stuff. Don't say there aren't any, because I'm sure there is at least one!

Start boosting yourself with affirmations. You can find millions of positive quotes online; but I believe that if you create your own, they will be more personal and relatable. To make it easier for you, I have dedicated a chapter to affirmations.

I used to say to myself, *I am good with words, and words will help me go places.*

It's crucial to create your affirmations close to your life and goals. It's even more important to feel them, not just repeat the words.

When you work on boosting your confidence, you'll put yourself first. You may have been taught that putting your needs first is a form of selfishness. This unfortunate misconception has resulted in millions of unhappy people who believe that doing things for themselves is a bad thing.

For generations, people were instilled with the opinion that a selfless person cares more about others than themselves. A selfless person of this type must be a good person — such a person never heeds their own needs, wishes, or urges. They make the world a better place for others. But, this isn't quite the definition of a selfless person.

I remember watching a video using the example of oxygen masks in planes. The cabin crew instructs the passengers that, in case of emergency, to put the oxygen mask on yourself first and then on the children. A parent or guardian must be in good shape to take care of children in emergencies. That's a smart way to be selfless and helpful.

The same applies to anything else in life. If you're not happy on the inside, if you haven't accepted yourself, if everything you do is good for others but not for you — then how can you expect to feel content, confident and good about yourself?

People who lack self-acceptance and are continuously negative about life, feel constant injustice, and cannot see anything good about themselves cannot be a good person for other people (especially not for their closest ones).

We believe that we love ourselves enough, but it takes only a little scratch on the surface to realize that this love might not be enough. How can you know whether you love yourself?

It might be painful, but you have to look inside. We are our own worst critics and judges. Others don't criticize or judge us as much or as often as we judge ourselves.

Why? We thrive for some perfection that cannot be achieved in real life, forgetting that we are perfect beings just the way we are.

While you think over and over why you said something, the other person has already forgotten about your words. You spend half of your day criticizing yourself because you made a mistake that was not that bad, instead of focusing on the things you do right.

To accept yourself means to accept your flaws. It means to admit that you're not always going to say or do the right thing. You're a human being, and we all make mistakes. It's not only normal but probable that we will make many of them. Remember, by preventing yourself from making a mistake, you're preventing yourself from living your life.

The moment you begin to forgive yourself and accept that you are a flawed human being is when your chains will start snapping. If you analyze your past actions and mental state, you'll see that any time you criticize yourself or beat yourself up over your choices or even small mistakes, weak confidence and fear, you're just adding another ring to your chain.

CHAPTER 2 – THE IMPORTANCE OF ACCEPTANCE

To help yourself in the process of self-acceptance and to start working on becoming who you want to be as a person, I have a few suggestions for you.

• Trust yourself. I always tell people to pay attention to their intuition. Often, we ignore it when it tries to tell us something. Every human being is intuitive. This knowledge kept our ancestors alert and saved them from many dangers in the past. Today, we live quite a safe life (free of risks that a wild animal might attack us, for example). We have technology that eases our living and makes everything within reach of our phone or computer. If you dedicate time to strengthen your intuition — just like your confidence, it exists in you and needs a little boosting — you'll soon realize that your gut feeling is always right.

Call it however you want — intuition, gut instinct, sacred knowledge — but this inner feeling that tells you when something isn't right, or that a person's energy does not work with you, shouldn't be ignored. How many times have you done something or went somewhere even when you did not feel like doing it?

• Learn to say no without feeling guilty. Most of us are taught that no is a bad word, people don't accept it as an answer, and the refusal to do something for someone else is considered bad manners. It will take you some time to learn how to say no without feeling like you are doing something wrong. Saying no is a healthy way of protecting yourself from living the life someone else creates for you (even if it is a simple thing that does not work for you). It will teach you to accept your values and beliefs, and protect you from doing things that drain your energy, waste your time, and fill you with negative emotions. Next time someone asks you to do something, even if this person is close to you, don't hesitate to say no. Don't use phrases like "Sorry, I don't think I can," "I will see/let you know later," or other excuses. Saying no is one of the highest forms of self-love. I always tell my clients, if you say "Yes" to something that you don't want to do, then you are saying "No" to yourself.

• Write down all the things about yourself you consider successful. When people are asked to list their accomplishments, they usually say one or two things (college, job), while forgetting to mention the ten other things. People often tend to consider the things they do every day as little or unimportant. To smile when you don't feel like smiling is an accomplishment. Going through your tough day at work, when you would instead prefer to go home and sleep, is an accomplishment. Quitting junk food is an accomplishment. Don't be modest; write down everything about you that makes you proud and fills you with joy.

• Baby steps out of the comfort zone. I know, I know — getting out of the cozy comfort zone can be a tough thing to do. When you face fear and anxiety, you cannot imagine yourself doing something different from your routine. I'm sure you've read and heard every saying about stepping out of the comfort zone already — and they are correct. I suggest you do this slowly (especially if you have anxiety) so you won't cause yourself disturbances and turbulences that will create more damage than good.

• Treat yourself. Start by doing things that you usually don't do. Use your list with things that you care about and that make you happy. You can start treating yourself, without having to wait for your friends or family to join you. So what if none of your friends want to go to the cinema, for instance? Buy yourself a ticket and go by yourself. You think it's silly and people will look at you as weird? No, people will not even notice that a person came to the movies by themselves. Thousands of people at this very moment are going to the movies alone and enjoying their time out!

Take yourself on a date. I know it sounds like a cliché, but once you sit down at that table by yourself without staring at your phone, you'll realize how liberating it feels. Enjoy the meal you ordered in peace, without having to fill in the silence with small talk. This is one of the best ways to start enjoying your own company. You will learn that you are enough and that doing things for yourself is one of the best things you can do for yourself.

• Travel if you can. Go by yourself or with friends, as traveling is one of the best things to fill you with fresh energy and help you unwind. It does not have to be somewhere far — it might be enough to go to another town. The change of scenery, getting out of your comfort zone, and spending less time in front of your computer or scrolling through social media is a wonderful thing for your brain. It feels like a massage to a sore muscle.

CHAPTER 2 – THE IMPORTANCE OF ACCEPTANCE

If you're traveling alone, it will be a whole new level of self-acceptance to do things you want to do. You won't have to compromise — get up when you want, go to this museum, that restaurant, spend the entire day in the park, or stay in bed. The itinerary is entirely up to you. You'll learn that you're capable of many great things — you'll have to organize everything, take care of yourself, learn to read maps, speak a foreign language, etc. The more you learn about yourself, the more you see that you can do things by yourself, the more you accept yourself as a capable, smart, and adequate person. It is an excellent confidence booster.

• Learn something new. As mentioned in the previous chapter, setting a new goal can boost your confidence. Allowing your brain to learn something new can be a smart way to move the focus on something else. When you're learning something new, there isn't much time left to overthink, analyze, criticize, or seek for imperfection. It will be an intentional defocusing because you are aware enough that you need to quit this pattern of beating yourself up. On the good side, you'll learn something new such as a foreign language, craft, or earn a new college degree, and you'll improve your self-image.

• It's time to take care of yourself. Taking care of yourself is self-love, self-acceptance, and self-awareness. If you don't do it, nobody else will. Taking care of yourself can come in many forms — hydration, eating healthy, seeing your doctor regularly, going places that you want to go, giving yourself credit for the things you do, shutting down your inner critic, meditation, or exercise. Doing things that are good for you will teach you how to love and accept yourself as a person with needs, dreams, goals, and talents.

• Learn to let go. Humans are prone to keeping their focus on the things they cannot control or are not able to change. It isn't the most natural thing in the world to let go of people, feelings, or situations that you cannot change. You hold on to them either out of habit or because you believe that you can change things. Holding on to such things is a significant reason for constant worrying, feeling as if you are stuck, and that only bad things are happening. Part of self-acceptance is to be able to see when things need to be released.

Let me give you an example: When you send your CV to a company, it's no use for you to worry and be on edge about whether they will call you. You sent in your application, and now it's time to let go — it isn't within your control if they call you for an interview. Instead of wasting your time worrying, hoping, and waiting — have fun, treat yourself in any way that works for you, and free your mind. Have the attitude of content — if they call you, great. If they don't, you'll still be fine.

• Stick to people whose energy feels good. Nobody wants to be around constant complainers and people who criticize every move you make. There must be at least one person in your life that has pleasant energy that feels good. I know it can be tough to go through life without support, which is why it is essential to find people you can be open with and who can support you.

• Silence your inner critic. We all have an inner critic whose voice is sometimes too loud and whose remarks are extreme and painful. Often the inner critic is hidden under the mask of rational thinking. But, your inner critic can make mistakes and convince you of things that are not true. You fed your inner critic for years by comparing yourself to others, accepting other people's truths, lies, and ways of being as the ultimate and best ways. Your inner critic is only alive because you still haven't accepted yourself. This critic wants you to be consistently dissatisfied with your life and choices. However, your inner critic is nothing but your ego's old beliefs that are trying to survive.

The moment you let your ego fall in the shadows and allow your soul to awaken is when you'll start accepting yourself. Your inner critic will start losing its voice. To silence your inner critic, you'll have to set a goal to accept yourself — the highest goal. This will require you to educate yourself on this topic (meditation, reading, forgiving yourself, giving gratitude for being here and alive, being content with what you have while you work to achieve something). One day you'll be powerful enough to observe the quiet echo of your inner critic's voice, and you'll smile, knowing that these thoughts no longer define you. You will know who you are!

• Fake it till you make it. I always laugh at this quote, but it's quite a method for tricking your mind. I don't recommend that you do illegal

CHAPTER 2 — THE IMPORTANCE OF ACCEPTANCE

things to accept yourself and boost your confidence. My suggestion is to start faking things that would not harm you or others. If speaking kind for yourself feels fake, fake it till you make it.

Say you feel the urge to start complaining, but, instead, you don't use a single complaining word. You are faking it, but you are making it, and so let this be your placebo effect. One day you'll no longer have to fake it. I always tell my clients about the story of when I wanted to leave my job. I would walk in every day pretending it was my last week. I would go around smiling from ear to ear, and if someone said, "Sharon, you look so happy today," I would say thank you... but in my head, I would be saying, "Ya, it's my last week." It did not take long for it to become a reality after that.

How to Make Your Self-Acceptance Bigger and Better

I've mentioned several methods that will help you accept yourself and improve your confidence. But this process won't happen just because you decided to do it. It requires your effort and will, and above all, your dedication to change your thoughts, the way you see yourself, and your environment.

1. Self-Awareness

It's our nature to seek tools to help us escape our reality for a little while. People always had their ways to do this, whether by reading newspapers or books, going to the cinema, playing video games or by religiously staring at their smartphones. Drinking, drugs, cigarettes, and even other people is a form of escapism that prevents people from becoming self-aware. No matter how useful social media is today, most people use it to create a different reality for themselves, their virtual friends, and followers. Although escaping our reality isn't a dangerous thing and helps us go through life, it should happen in moderation.

Self-awareness isn't a fairytale, and we humans know it. We always go for the next thing that will take our attention off our rough reality. Living without any distraction means an inevitable facing of our thoughts, our minds, emotions, and what we have achieved so far.

But, it can be a step out of the comfort zone. It can be the danger you need to face, the fear you have to overcome to become immune and see things as they are.

The more aware you become of yourself, the more you'll be able to accept that this is you.

You can have the best gadgets in the world, jump from one relationship to another, indulge in food and drinks, but at one point you'll have to look inside yourself.

Self-awareness is the road that leads to self-acceptance. It is quite bumpy and not very pleasant, but once you walk it, it won't be so scary anymore. You will feel and detect your pain and insecurities, but also your skills and talents. Self-awareness will teach you some valuable lessons. Once you are aware of yourself, your mind will serve you memories you thought were long forgotten. You will be able to see the patterns you created to survive clearly. Also, you'll be able to realize when people manipulate you. You will understand when people did their best to protect you or love you even if you were not completely aware of that at the moment.

2. Self-Regulation

People whose self-acceptance is on a high level are aware of the fact that they have control over their thoughts and emotions as well.

Once you become who you are and observe your emotions, thoughts, achievements in life, strengths, skills, weak sides, and failures, you're ready to start regulating what goes through your head.

Self-regulation does not mean you suppress your emotions; au contraire, it means that you only recognize them for what they are — emotions. Emotions are energy in motion; temporary things that do not define you.

Here is my favourite method for silencing my inner critic. When my inner critic starts raising its voice (creating feelings of self-hatred that threatens to ruin my self-acceptance and confidence), I think of three great things about myself. Three great things against one negative thought. Who's winning?

If you find this to be challenging, it's because you still struggle with your self-acceptance. Don't beat yourself up about it because the fact that some people need more time to accept themselves can be a subconscious thing, which is when we go to the next option.

3. Self-Transcendence

Transcendence means to rise above to something higher. In this case, self-transcendence means to rise from the self to your higher self.

You, like everyone else, have a higher self which is part of something more substantial, part of the whole, the universe. By this logic, we are all one, and we are all connected.

Self-transcendence puts the divine in us, allowing us to see that God, the Universe, or the Source lies in us. We shouldn't seek some miraculous power outside of us.

Becoming self-transcendent, or opening your eyes to this truth can be done with the help of meditations. Ten to twenty minutes of meditation per day will help you clean your mind, allow you to learn to observe your thoughts, and become strong enough to select which thoughts are useful for you. It will help you become selective about the quality of your mind.

The more you meditate, and the more you cleanse your entire being, you'll feel the need of consuming clean food. You'll see that the material things you no longer use only clutter your space. You are raising your vibration, which even if you are not aware, will select the people in your life. Those who vibrate lower will disappear from your life.

Your self-awareness becomes sharper, and self-regulation will become your favourite habit. Once you activate these two, you can say that you have become self-transcendent.

What do you gain if you become self-transcendent?

1. A shift in your focus. You will understand yourself better. When you know yourself, you'll understand others. So, if your focus used to be you and your flaws, as your focus widens, it moves to others as

well. You become more considerate and kinder to others, and you'll want to share your knowledge with others. The world needs people who are awakened to this point where they can selflessly help others — once they've helped themselves!

2. Change of values. If before self-awareness, self-regulation, and self-transcendence, your values mostly related to your old ways of thinking, now they will change. You will be content with yourself, and the essential reward is your acceptance. Other people's validation and approval will no longer be important to you.

3. You will want to do what is right. Not only for you, but everyone else, including animals, plants, and the planet. Self-transcendent people lack selfishness — they think twice before cutting a tree because they need wood to make a chair, for instance. They are concerned about animals and their rights, but also care for nature across the world. They want things to be suitable for everyone because they know we are all one.

One of my favourite methods of self-transcendence is transcendental meditation. Writing a journal can be of great help, even if writing isn't your strongest skill. Writing your thoughts and emotions will serve as a valve. Write how you feel, write about your dreams and your feelings, and notice how you feel afterwards. Often, writing will liberate you from emotional tension and chaos of thoughts.

I am also a huge fan of mindfulness meditation. It is one of the most powerful meditations that teach us to stay in the present moment. According to it, the time is always now, and the past and the future don't exist. Mindfulness meditation can make your anxiety disappear. We tend to get anxious because we either create impossible outcomes for the future, which only causes our bodies to excrete cortisol, the stress hormone.

We spend too much time analyzing our past. We think of the mistakes, choices, and decisions we made, the people we let hurt us. This is how depression and sadness kick in.

When you become self-transcendent, and more in control of yourself, your thoughts, and your actions, you live in the present moment. To be fully aware of the moment you are in, you'll have to turn off your

CHAPTER 2 – THE IMPORTANCE OF ACCEPTANCE

autopilot. Think of the times you ate your lunch without even noticing the flavours, or when you were taking money out of the ATM or commuting to work. In situations like these, we often go on autopilot. We are too busy thinking of other things, rehearsing what we shall say, what we should have done better, whether our future is good or not. And while we are busy living in the past or future, the present moment passes and never returns. To be mindful means to stay here and now, without missing a minute of your life.

Acceptance is crucial in building your confidence and self-esteem. Since I work with children and adults, I see that we need to start working from the very foundation, which is why I always tell parents and people who plan to have children — teach your children to accept themselves from the earliest childhood.

Children will only accept themselves as much as their parents accept them. Some parents are not aware of this and tend to instill self-doubt and feelings of inadequacy in their children, who grow up believing that when others accept them, they will feel better, more loved, more adequate, and more important.

I always emphasize (because I now know) that happiness is tightly connected with self-acceptance. The root of all unhappiness, depression, and the urge to be loved and approved by everyone can be found in the simple fact that the person is still not in touch with their "self" nor have they passed through the rough path called self-awareness. Even the ones who are willing to become self-aware may become very frightened of everything they learn in this process. So they shut that door and hardly ever return.

We must be brave and fearless to see who we are, what makes us feel that way, why we allow people to hurt us, and why we agree with the negative things we say to ourselves, and why we agree with the negative things other people say about us.

You will notice that you accept yourself by merely allowing yourself to be happy. People who cannot allow happiness in their lives don't believe they deserve it. Somewhere deep in their mind, they think that they are not good or perfect enough to be happy, have beautiful things, go places, or get the job of their dreams.

Compassion isn't meant only for the others. It's of far greater importance for yourself. You have to learn to forgive yourself. Forgiving is part of letting go. Holding a grudge against yourself is like drinking poison every day, expecting to improve your health.

In this case, there is no placebo effect — you are punishing yourself with negative self-talk; you allow your inner critic to scream on a megaphone, while you sit helplessly listening and nodding. Perhaps it kills you, but you were taught, and you convinced yourself that you cannot do anything and that this is who you are now.

I was this person. I know how this feels. Deep down, you know that you can change things, but first, you have to free yourself from all the unnecessary burdens you are willingly holding. It isn't helping you out, it only adds physical pain, and now it is time for you to rise.

To start loving yourself and see the good in you and be able to forgive yourself about everything you did that was not beneficial for you, you'll first have to realize that you don't have any obligation to show your worthiness to other people. It isn't your obligation to perform a play in front of them, hoping they will see the kind, loving, and worthy person you are. Be yourself, and if someone notices that you are a decent person, then it is all right. If not, trust me, you'll survive.

See this process like building a house. (I love this house example thing.) You work on building a lovely house, with a nice garden, beautiful interior, protective rooftop, and you plant trees and flowers in your garden. But this place is a home for you and you only. You are not building this house hoping that someone would find it lovely enough to knock on the door and tell you how perfect your home is. If someone does that, then great, thank them and invite them in for a cup of tea or coffee. But, if no one knocks on your door, that's fine as well. Continue living in this lovely home without hoping or worrying why no people are coming over. And remember that this is your only home.

So, what stops you from starting today?

Next time you have a feeling like you are not good enough, stop this thought and ask yourself, Would I say this to my younger self? Would I say this to a child?

CHAPTER 2 — THE IMPORTANCE OF ACCEPTANCE

You must understand that you are the only one with that DNA combo in this world. There is no one else who looks like you, talks like you, or walks like you. You are an authentic and unique human being.

If you believe that you won't be able to go through this, take me as an example — I lived through a numbing depression and had to face my brother's suicide, asking myself questions that did not have answers. This hit me so hard that I tried to do the same (twice), and was not able to see all the things I am now writing. Nights out, alcohol, and silence were my way of escaping reality.

Sometimes we need to go through the ugliest corners of ourselves to learn that there must be another way that leads out of the darkness. This is when we start walking towards the light, the path of healing, forgiveness, and acceptance of our uniqueness, qualities, and who we are as a person. Only in this way can we see that all our difficult times were hidden blessings (which we were not able to see at that moment), in that they served to push us out of our comfort zone.

CHAPTER 3

Mindfulness

We have come to the third chapter, where I will write about one of my favourite ways to improve your confidence, thoughts, and life. People often misunderstand mindfulness. I am not saying this because I want to make it look like rocket science. But it seems like mission impossible for people who tend to live in the past or the future.

To be mindful means to be entirely here at the present moment, completely aware of what you are doing, where you are, what you say, eat, or feel. Mindfulness is often perceived as a thing we are all capable of doing. I get questions like, "Aren't we all mindful all the time?" or, "I am mindful, I mind my own business," or, "What do you mean it takes some practice to be aware?"

These questions are how I know that people are not entirely aware of the meaning of the word, or of the action itself.

I am dedicating a whole chapter to mindfulness because it's one of the crucial things you can do to help yourself overcome depression and anxiety, which are often connected with our worries for the future, overthinking and analyzing our past, and fear of the things that we are supposed to go through.

To be mindful, you need to make a decision that you won't let your mind wander into your past. You'll have to be aware when you catch your thoughts creating a cluster of worries or crazy scenarios for the future. The moment you realize such things are going through your mind is when you become aware and in control of your thoughts;

that moment when you willingly bring yourself into the moment and place your focus on what you are doing right then and there.

Mindfulness isn't complicated, but some people believe that it cannot be achieved since the mind creates a stream of thoughts that we are not able to stop or quiet.

Anyone can be mindful. Anyone can do it, and all it takes is a little practice.

Before I continue with the ways that will help improve your mindfulness, I want to point out a few myths.

Mindfulness has nothing to do with religion, and being mindful does not disturb your beliefs. Originally, mindfulness was taught by Buddha, but even then, it had nothing to do with changing or instilling specific ideas. Its only purpose is to help you become more aware of the moment you live in and teach you to live in it without waiting, planning, and expecting some moment in the future.

Another myth is that mindfulness is a piece of cake. Even though anyone can do it, mindfulness can be quite a challenge. If you want to be better at something, you need to spend more time practising. People believe that once they've decided to become mindful, that they could do it. Maybe some people can, but the percentage is small.

To improve your mindfulness, you need to practice little by little. The best way is to practice mindfulness meditation. You can start with any meditation if you want to train your mind to stillness. Meditation, in general, is an excellent way to learn how to observe your thoughts by seeing them as words on a dark screen. Once you realize that your mind produces thousands of thoughts per day (sometimes even unconnected words that mean nothing), you'll be able to cut any thought that threatens to grow into something more substantial. Of course, I speak about negative thoughts that don't serve your well-being.

Meditation is perhaps the best way to start your mindfulness training, but it isn't the only tool that will help you be more mindful. To be mindful, you need to set the intention to be. For example, before you start your day, set an intention to be mindful of the things you are going to do. When you wash your face, pay attention

CHAPTER 3 – MINDFULNESS

to the feeling of water on your skin. Smell the soap. Focus on the feeling that the toothbrush gives your gums, teeth, and tongue. Pay attention to the taste of your toothpaste. Then, continue your day by being entirely in the moment — focus on the taste of your coffee and breakfast.

Notice how you no longer pay attention to the time small activities take. When I am not mindful, I catch myself thinking that I am losing time when I wait in line. Or I feel anxious to finish faster the small things I have to do or have my coffee more quickly. This is anxiety, to jump faster in the next moment, seeing the current one as not exciting enough, or as a moment that is on your way to something better.

When you start your mindfulness practices, you'll learn to slow down. And what happens when we slow down? We become calmer, of course, more aware of where we are now, and that the moment we are in isn't that bad, even if it is only a minute or two while we are brushing our teeth.

We have so many things that are made to ruin the mindfulness that, sometimes it seems like a constant battle against them. Being mindful of your phone in your hand while eating lunch is undoubtedly a tough challenge — you are distracting yourself from paying attention to your food, and how it makes you feel.

People often ask me why I talk about mindfulness like it is something great and exciting when, according to my own words it means to be aware of every moment, even if things are not going well.

I agree, not every present moment is fantastic. Life brings moments that we will want to escape. Speaking from personal experience, I know what it means to want to avoid reality and hide. Life isn't always peace and joy, but that does not mean that we should avoid the present moment, hoping and waiting for the next one. The next moment will come, and that moment too might not be the nicest. So what are we going to do? Skip it with a distraction and wait for the next, and the one after that one, and so on?

Mindfulness teaches us to pay attention, even when things are not going smoothly. To be fully present in all moments means that you are making peace with the situation. I know that this sounds like giving up and staying inactive to change, but it isn't like that.

When you are present in the moment, even if it isn't a pleasant one, you learn to accept life in a friendly manner. Since mindfulness teaches us that every moment is different from another, and those moments constantly change, facing the not-so-pleasant present can be a real lesson. Things change, and therefore there is no need for worrying, as when you worry you don't live in the moment. It is also a lesson that some things in life must be faced no matter how much we don't want to.

Mindfulness isn't a passive thing. Sure, it has to do with our mind and observing what we feel, do, taste, or say at that moment, but it is quite an activity. It is the most important activity to watch and learn how your mind reacts to the current happenings. It taught me how much I hold on to specific moments that feel good and make me laugh. I understood that the pleasant moments made me wish for them to last a little longer, but also that I wanted to get out of the bad moments immediately.

You might say, "Big deal." But, without mindfulness, you are not able to realize that there is no way out of the bad moments or a way to extend the pleasant ones. You only can go through them fully aware of what is happening, knowing that "this too shall pass."

Mindfulness will open your eyes to your attachments to pleasant moments. When we hold to the moment that we felt amazing, we do nothing but relive the memories. That moment is gone. I don't say that we should avoid reminiscence, but holding on to those moments when life isn't giving you easy times, is living in the past. You create a habit to see the present as negative, and such practice makes you feel dissatisfied with your life.

When you start practising your mindfulness, you are not only not missing out on your life, but you learn to let go of the habits of holding on to memories or resisting to allow yourself to be fully present in your not so pleasant present.

Once you learn to let go, you get rid of the weight that causes you pain. Letting go is a relief you did not know you needed. Without the

CHAPTER 3 – MINDFULNESS

burden of memories from the past, or worries about the future, you feel at ease with yourself and your life. You don't expect anything, and that feeling of lightness opens you for more options. As they say, when nothing happens, anything is possible.

Mindfulness Tips

If you decide to become mindful of your life, I have a few helpful tips that will ease the process for you.

When I started my mindfulness journey, I decided that I needed to be more aware of the things and people in my life, but also for every achievement, even when my days were not so good.

Naturally, you are aware of the people in your life, and you use the things you have at home or work, but how mindful are you of them? Most people (even if they are not even aware of it) take much for granted.

You feel like having a glass of water, and you don't think twice about how life without it would feel. You turn on the tap and let it run because you like it cold. There is no awareness that your life will be a real struggle if you didn't have access to clean water.

Your friends and family are always forgiving and helpful, but you barely acknowledge this with words or actions, because you don't think of it at all. But these people have feelings, and one day they might not be around anymore.

Taking things for granted is a real mindfulness killer, which is why I suggest that you start giving gratitude for people and things in your life.

Starting from today, dedicate a few minutes of your day to thank God, or the Universe, or life (whatever you connect with) for your family, friends, co-workers, that stranger that helped you with your bags, the pleasant lady at the bank, and everyone who made your day better. You can give gratitude even to people who made your day lame because this way they taught you what kind of person you don't want to be or have in your life.

RADIATE CONFIDENCE – Sharon Ledwith

Be grateful for every little thing you own from your socks to your car. Some people can only dream of having half the stuff you own.

Be grateful for your bed, your job, the bills (it means you can pay them), your bathroom, computer, phone, internet, the food in your fridge.

Thank yourself for enduring the day, for graduating, for landing the job you have, for the dedication you have for achieving your goals.

Once you spend several minutes thanking for every blessing in your life, you'll feel better. As people say, count your blessings.

If you feel like you'll forget to do this, you can always start writing a gratitude diary. Get a journal only for this activity and write down all the things for which you are grateful. To keep the habit flowing, set a goal to write three things about which you feel thankful.

In one month, you'll have a new habit, and your entire mindset will change because your focus will change from being focused on the things you lack. Your mind will shift to see all the things that work for you, all the people that make your life amazing, and all the things you have achieved.

You can create any method that will help you in your gratitude process. You can turn your social media in your visual gratitude diary, but if this seems less private for you, you can always turn to other ideas. I have created gratitude jars with the children I teach. People who use these jars (they slip a piece of paper with written things every day), say at the end of the year they open it and read all the things they were grateful for. It makes them realize that they are ending the year in an abundance of love, support, and good health.

When you work on your gratitude, you are learning to be more aware of the things you like in your life; a method that will improve your general well-being, state of mind and will help you become mindful much easier.

The second method I recommend to increase your mindfulness is the method of breathing. Breathing is something we do without effort. We barely pay attention to our breath, without knowing that

CHAPTER 3 — MINDFULNESS

conscious breathing can help us get rid of headaches, anxiety, relax us, and help us fall asleep.

Most people connect deep breathing with meditation or yoga, but you don't have to practice either to give yourself a few minutes of your day to breathe deeply and intentionally.

Usually, in meditation, deep breathing is suggested at the very beginning. The reason behind this is because deep breaths are beneficial for total body relaxation.

How is breathing connected with mindfulness?

Let's say you don't meditate, but you decide to relax before sleep, and you want to give deep conscious breathing a try.

Lie down and inhale deeply. In this process, you are very mindful of your focus. The only place your attention goes to is your lungs. Your mind is free of any thoughts. Perhaps you wonder how you'll achieve this if you don't have a meditation practice.

Remember, your only interest in this moment of deep breathing is how your stomach rises up and down. Notice the air going from your nostrils to your lungs. Then you hold the breath for a few seconds (count to three) and then slowly breathe it all out. During the exhaling, remain aware only of the feeling — notice how your lungs are emptying, feel your diaphragm moving, and the release of air leaving your body.

You don't need more than five to ten minutes per day. It is a perfect method with powerful benefits. You will practice your mindfulness (your focus does not wander to anything other than your breathing), and you are cleansing your body from stale energy while renewing your cells with fresh oxygen.

Deep breathing will relax you if you want to sleep, but also will clear your head, and help you feel lighter during your challenging days.

We often forget to breathe consciously, which is why you'll often hear people saying they feel tired, fatigued, and sleepy, and then wonder why this is happening when they've eaten and slept well.

Shallow breaths, sitting in unnatural positions, being inside all day long, are the reasons why people feel unwell. They barely pay attention to their breathing.

Naturally, you can't go through your entire day while breathing deeply. But you can dedicate a few minutes a day to it. Once you try it, you'll want to create a habit of conscious diaphragm breathing. There is no better way to experience the present moment than when you sit down and breathe.

Now, we finally got to the mindfulness meditation part.

For some people, the word meditation awakens uneasy emotions. They firmly believe (another limiting belief) that they are not made for something as calm and as peaceful as meditation.

Before you claim that you are too temperamental, unsteady, lively, or active for meditation, let me tell you a few things.

It is a challenge for everyone. At first, we all believe that we can't do it. We are afraid of whether we are doing it right. Then we face the unavoidable need to adjust, scratch, open our eyes to look around.

There is no perfect way of meditating. It depends on you. When you decide to spend the next ten minutes in meditation, the first thing you'll "face" is your mind. Suddenly, you are "attacking" it with doing nothing. You intend to direct your focus to your breathing. Your mind will "fight," or try its best, to give you at least ten thoughts that are supposed to take away your attention. And this is the trick that you have to do to "win" this battle.

Once you sit or lay down to meditate, you have to know that it is entirely normal to become aware of everything. Sounds, your position, how your breath feels, thousands of words and thoughts that occur will try to steal your attention.

It is all right. See your thoughts as a natural stream that never ends. Instead of holding on to a thought and giving it the power to distract you, welcome it, and let it go.

While you are sitting or lying down, your mind is serving you thoughts about your day at work. Or it digs up memories you have

CHAPTER 3 – MINDFULNESS

forgotten. Perhaps you think about crazy stuff like where you have put your passport.

Allow these thoughts to pass through your head, without sticking to any of it. Even if that occurs, slowly return your focus to your breath.

How to Do the Mindfulness Meditation

If you are a first-time meditator, you can find a guided mindfulness meditation that will help you go through the process. You won't have to worry whether you stayed in the meditative state long enough, whether you breathed well, or if you focused on the right things.

Mindfulness meditation can be done even without a vocal guide — it takes just five to ten minutes of your day. Set a time when you'll slow down and relax. It could be the first thing in the morning, or right before you go to sleep.

It is essential to do it when nobody disturbs you. Put your phone on silent, or leave it in another room.

You can choose to sit down, or lay down if that is more comfortable. My suggestion is to pick a chair where you'll have your back straight and your feet on the floor. You can do this in your office, at home or even on a bench in the park.

Wherever your meditation place is, keep in mind that you need to keep your back in a comfortable straight position. Do not hunch, or sit in a position that would give you cramps or back pain.

If you have already practised yoga or meditation, feel free to sit in a cross-legged position. Your arms can be placed on top of your knees, in your lap, or by your side — whatever is comfortable for you.

Now that you have found your position, make your final adjustments before you continue. Some people like focusing their gaze on an object. You can look in the distance, focus on the flame of a candle, or on the floor.

I find it easier to meditate with my eyes closed.

Now relax, and stay in this position for a few moments, without any intention, expectations, worries. Just stay like this, breathing normally.

Slowly bring your focus to your breathing. This means that your attention goes to your lungs and how they fill with air. Notice how the breath feels — notice how the inhale massages your internal organs. Hear the sound of breathing in and breathing out.

If you find it challenging to keep your focus on your breathing, you can say it in your mind. Focus on your words "breathing in" when you inhale, and "breathing out" when you exhale. Let these phrases be your focal point. With time you'll learn to focus even without them.

Just breathe. Nothing else is important at this moment. You don't have to be anywhere in the next ten minutes. Your attention is solely dedicated to your breath, its freshness, and how it changes your physical body.

Notice how every deep inhalation slowly relaxed your muscles — feel how this breath of fresh air goes into your body. Imagine how this breath goes to the place where you feel any pain, anxiousness, or even cramps. It may be your stomach, shoulders, knees. Breathe in and "send" the breath to these places.

With time, your attention might start wandering. External sounds might "steal" it, or perhaps your stream of thoughts might become more dominant. It is normal, and it is all right if it happens. Do not worry whether you are doing this meditation the right way. You are doing it perfectly well.

As you notice your thoughts occurring, or external noise stealing your attention, return your focus to your breathing.

It should be done easily, without feeling that you are making a mistake. Just like when you return your attention to the screen when you watch a film, once you hear a noise coming from the outside.

Some people might not be able to focus on their breathing and will experience their mind wandering through the entire meditation.

CHAPTER 3 – MINDFULNESS

But this is a regular thing. It will teach you mindfulness as well. Just continue sitting in your position with your eyes closed or open, keep breathing, and observe your thoughts. Don't engage in them, simply "watch" them come and go. It is a beautiful exercise to become mindful of your thoughts. You will realize how your mind "produces" thoughts that are not connected. In fact, you'll notice how most of these so-called thoughts are only words — literally, a flood of words.

Sometimes, when I have my mindfulness meditation, I get to observe words and thoughts that make me laugh because they have no connection whatsoever. It means that I am only an observer, not a contributor. I don't hold onto or linger on my thoughts — I don't analyze why they appeared in my mind. Rather, I just see them just as I see film credits rolling on a dark screen.

And the most significant benefit of these types of wandering thoughts during mindfulness meditation is that you'll soon become quickly aware of thoughts that are not serving you.

With enough practice, you'll be able to detect worrying, negative, limiting thoughts. Instead, give them the attention they want, you'll "see" their appearance, won't do a thing about them and will let them dissolve in your mind.

This is how you learn that our emotions are born from our thoughts. The more we stick to a thought, especially if it is a worrying thought, the more we enhance it, the more it changes our chemistry, creating feelings of anxiety, worry, inadequacy, sadness, or unworthiness.

If a simple worrying thought (that usually happens as a scenario that has a low chance of becoming real) could shift us in a negative state, imagine what your mind can do if you push it to focus on the things you want to do. With the focus on the right thoughts, you could change your entire health state, beliefs, and state of mind. Just imagine how if you give your attention to positive outcomes, then your body will start to react positively — instead of the stress hormone cortisol, it will begin secreting dopamine.

As I said, your mind does not know what is real. If your negative thinking can make you cry, worry or even sick for a situation that hasn't happened yet (and might not even happen at all), just imagine what beautiful change you can do with your mind and body if you learn how to select your thoughts and give attention only to those that make you feel well.

I often get asked what to do when you feel like moving or scratching during a meditation. Many people resist movements, but I allow them. Beginners but also people with experience in meditations learn and know that you need to stay calm during your meditative state. We are just human beings, and, naturally, we might feel like adjusting. Our legs might feel itchy, or we might feel like sneezing or coughing.

Holding yourself from scratching or moving, might cause you even more significant discomfort. Your focus will shift immediately to this thing (itchy leg for an example), and no matter how strong your mind is, you won't be able to ignore this. So, while you meditate, give knowledge that you are going to stop for a little bit so that you can adjust yourself, scratch, or sneeze.

As your meditation comes to its end, don't just jump up and continue with your day. You have intentionally calmed yourself down and had your focus on only one thing. Slowly move your toes, hands, and shoulders. Allow external noises to be part of your attention again. Inhale deeply and slowly open your eyes (or shift your awareness back into the room).

And just like that, you practiced your ten-minute-or-so mindfulness meditation successfully.

You will know whether it was easy or difficult for you, but know that you need to be proud because you made a lovely change in your daily routine. If you decide to create a habit, you are already winning.

The next thing you can do, besides breathing and meditation, is to become more selective about your thoughts. With more meditation, you'll be able to become just an observer of your thoughts easily. And when you observe, without engaging in this process, you see the bigger picture. This way, you'll be able to select your thoughts. As I mentioned earlier, when you meditate and have your attention "slip" and start wandering all over the place, you can easily observe

CHAPTER 3 – MINDFULNESS

your thoughts and see that very often they are nothing but unconnected words.

To be selective with your thoughts is to be mindful. And to be mindful of your thoughts means that you are aware enough which thoughts serve you well. Perhaps now it seems like a crazy impossible thing, but, trust me, it does not take a lot of practising to be able to detect which thoughts are right for you.

Of course, this too is individual, but most people are capable of detecting the thoughts that are not good for them. Once you do it, you start to select them. *A-ha, so this thought is about to grow into worry or overthinking. This thought won't make me feel well at all. And this thought is meaningless, and I see no reason why I should let it through my mind.*

You learn what is right for you. Consciously, you are doing a good thing for you — a thought process that is carefully selected so that it will improve your mental state, your self-acceptance, and your confidence.

If you are not sure whether this method is going to be easy, you can always ask yourself, *"Is this thought going to make me feel good or bad?"* That too is a form of awareness.

Another method that I love to practice is the method of doing nothing. Living in a busy world where it is expected from us to be on time, be productive at work, pay attention to our family members and friends, can be a real challenge. And this challenge often results in stress.

People tend to see being busy or stressed as a way of productivity. But I don't like the whole idea of being busy and stressed.

Yes, I know that a stressful situation cannot always be avoided — but at least we can do something to soothe the negativity stress causes.

The art of doing nothing is my favourite thing to do in super busy days. Now, I don't say that you should sit down and do nothing for five hours, but everybody has ten to fifteen minutes when they can do nothing. By nothing, I don't mean scrolling on Facebook, Instagram, reading tweets, or thinking about your day.

I mean not doing anything at all.

Allow your brain to relax for ten to fifteen minutes. As in the meditation, let yourself breathe normally, whenever a thought occurs, let it dissolve, and continue to observe your thoughts. If no thoughts occur (which can be real progress) then congratulations, you did it. You did nothing.

When I give myself these minutes of doing nothing, I learn that I like to observe. If I happen to be at the park or in a coffee shop or my favourite place, Lady's Well, I sit down, leave my phone in my bag and watch the world go by. I observe people passing by, cars driving, birds flying. I sit quietly and observe. No small talk, no staring at my phone, no reading, no music just doing nothing but watching.

So far, we talked about training your mind into mindfulness. But besides the mind, there is the body which we also use to communicate with people, show our emotions, interests, intentions, and what we feel.

Our body language communication is shown in various ways. How we shake hands, how we move our hands when we explain things, how we sit or stand, whether we look the other person in their eyes when we speak to them. It is all part of the body language. Some people tend to notice it, while others don't pay attention to it at all.

So how are body language and the way we use our physical body connected with mindfulness?

To be mindful about your body language means that you are fully aware of the way you hold your posture, how you move your hands if you see people in their eyes while talking to them.

Mindful body language will make you more aware of the way you move your body in communication with other people, and how it affects them. The moment you become aware of your body language, you become mindful of it. And just like that, your focus moves not only to your body language but to other people as well.

Suddenly you notice how people are walking, standing, talking with their arms, you observe their facial expressions, how long they look at other people in their eyes.

CHAPTER 3 – MINDFULNESS

If by now, you were not aware of your body language, now it is the time to start becoming more mindful about it.

Let's start with simple exercises such as you noticing how you speak to people. Are you facing them? Do you have a problem looking in their eyes? Do you use your hands a lot? Or, are you completely peaceful?

Just a little observation will give you a lot of answers. You can set a challenge to start looking at people you are speaking to, at the beginning you can choose someone you are comfortable with. People find looking in other people's eyes a bit uncomfortable because our eyes tend to speak more than our mouths. When you look someone in their eyes, you can show your vulnerability, fear, desire, anger, or hatred.

Another method you can use is the mirror effect. Stand in front of a mirror and start talking to yourself. I know it sounds funny, but it is a helpful method. Just talk about anything. See if you can say "I love you" to yourself. Talk about your emotions, what makes you happy, sad, angry.

Say to yourself things such as "I am lovable." If this feels odd and you feel silly, then this is a great indicator that you need to work on this area more. Your mirror is helping you become more mindful about your self-love, for example. Give this method a try, and you'll soon realize that it is quite easy and liberating. You will notice which areas of your life are still difficult for you — you'll be able to detect where your limiting beliefs lie and become aware of them instantly.

When you try, it might seem crazy and funny, but as you practice it more and more, it will become easier and you'll see how your words come out more smoothly. This method will help you open up more about your emotions when talking to other people, even to your therapist (if you have one). Later, when you communicate with others or speak about yourself, this method will come up to mind and you'll become mindful about the things you say and how you say them.

These exercises are not futile. They have the purpose of making you mindful not only for the things that go through your mind but also the way your thoughts and emotions affect your body.

We are often not aware of our nonverbal communication. And mindfulness is about everything we do, think, and say.

The more mindful you become about your body language and posture, the more you'll be able to decode other people's body language. Because, of course, you'll understand others if you know yourself.

Mindfulness body language will help you pick up other people's emotions and intentions, even if they don't say a word to you.

People tend to hide their words, but their body language (unless they are entirely mindful about it) will give them away. You will quickly know if a person is bored while talking to you. You can detect people lying. The great thing about it is that you'll be able to notice if the other person is interested in you, has a fun time talking to you, or is generally not interested in what you have to say.

Finally, you'll be able to pick up other people's emotions and what they hide behind their words (this could be a secondary benefit of being mindful). You will become aware when you are present at the moment in both mind and body and when you go autopilot.

There are countless cases where people do things mechanically (unlock the door, scroll through social media, eating or drinking, taking money out of the ATM, saying hello to their neighbours). It is a fact that our brain sometimes needs a break, but it can be a real danger. Not only because you are missing the present moment, but because you might end the day and not be able to remember whether you have locked the door, turned off the iron and things like that.

Today's world is forcing us to multitask, which is another over-romanticized thing that isn't benefiting us. You can't focus on doing five things at the same time — your focus will only stay on one or two, and the other three things will be done on autopilot. This isn't something that makes you powerful. Instead, it only drains your energy and forces you to be negative and barely be present at the moment.

CHAPTER 3 – MINDFULNESS

So, if your body language was not in your focus up till now, it is high time to observe the way you walk, where are your feet during a conversation, how often and how long you look people in the eye, where you keep your hands, what your voice sounds like when you talk to different people.

After everything you have read in this chapter, the only thing that you need to do is to start being more mindful. It does not take a day, a week, or a month to become mindful. It is something you need to do every day, even as little as a few minutes.

There are no rules or harsh training that will make you mindful within a specified period. Above all, you need to want to be more mindful because you want to live in the present and be aware of how you feel, speak, think (select your thoughts) and not just go through life doing things mechanically.

Am I in the mood to be mindful every day, all day? No, definitely not. But, I am always working on myself, and I allow myself the time to be mindful.

If one day I am entirely present in the moment, paying attention to my thoughts, the taste of the food I eat, the way I talk to people, or observe their body language, words, actions and how they carry themselves, the other day I simply cannot help but not do any of this.

But, still, the intention to be mindful is your fuel. You are not going to practice it every day because some days you'll be busy, not in the mood, or simply tired. But, just because you want to be more mindful, you can spend five or ten minutes per day just being in the present moment.

You can choose to do nothing as a form of relaxation and a break, but it will also be your brief mindful period. Another way to be mindful is by setting the intention to spend one minute (or set your own timing) during which you'll practice it.

Either use this time to slow down, do your meditation (with eyes closed or open, in your home, at the park, in the office) or just sit back and observe your thoughts.

There are millions of ways you can do this, and it is entirely up to you as to which method you should choose.

Focusing on one thing at a time helped me a lot in my mindfulness process. I gave up the idea that multitasking is a good thing. Sure, you can finish more chores, but where is your mind in the whole thing? I am no longer on autopilot. Mindfulness helps me be aware when I do small tasks, and later, I don't have to wonder whether I have done them or not.

When you focus on one thing, you are mindful but also respectful towards your activity. When you eat, focus on the flavour, the temperature of your food, the way the food makes you feel. Don't take your phone during your meals. Some cultures in the world consider it rude to bring your phone to your table. So, take that as an example, respect your own body and your mealtime. If it is hard for you to stay away from your phone (if, like me, for instance, working on it all day), start with small steps. Before you start eating, give gratitude for the food on your table, but also for your job because it pays you enough so you can afford food. This is one small step — gratitude is mindfulness.

Eating is just one example. Think of all the times when you were with your friends, and you or they were staring at the phone. It does not feel right when the person you are with is more interested to see the photos on Instagram, instead of paying attention to you. You cannot do both. Technically you can, but your focus will be absent from one of these things.

One thing at a time will relax your brain — it will give it time to pay attention to the situation or person it needs to give the attention to. When you have your mind relaxed, you don't tend to stress out. So, mindfulness methods bring you another benefit — less stress.

My mindfulness helped me in the process of weight loss. The intention and discipline are not the only things that help you go through a diet. Mindfulness is the Joker card.

When you observe your thoughts, you get to observe your urges as well. Instead, to react immediately once you feel a craving or

CHAPTER 3 – MINDFULNESS

wanting for something, you stay calm and see these "urges" for what they are — just thoughts.

Sure, feeling hungry is a real thing and you should never starve yourself, but when you are mindful enough, you tend to notice when your hunger comes out of boredom. Many people eat when they are not hungry (they are bored, want to fill a void, or eat out of habit), without even thinking that this hunger isn't real.

When you are mindful, you can easily detect that you feel a craving for a specific food. Your craving might have been initiated by a simple picture, an ad, or a thought that was not anyhow connected with your hunger.

So, once you observe and acknowledge the craving or urge, you get to notice whether your body reacts. If there is no physical reaction in your stomach, then you can be sure that this urge was nothing but a thought.

You become selective of your thoughts. As I mentioned earlier, our thoughts can change everything for us — emotions, intentions, determination, even ruin our diet.

Mindfulness is your key to understanding what thoughts (urges and desires) are right for you. When you observe them without engaging in the stream of thoughts you are entirely independent, and your own thoughts cannot manipulate you.

I know this sounds crazy, but it is true. I encourage you to test yourself and see how successful you'll be in this mindfulness practice.

When you start your mindfulness process and start observing your thoughts (with the help of meditation), you'll come to one fantastic discovery. Your inner critic is just an old record that is playing out loud, the same words over and over again. You will laugh at these words and phrases, not only because they are not valid and you finally see that, but because now you can take that record and let it go.

These limiting beliefs that were recorded and were played continuously will start to lose their loudness. Perhaps you'll break that record, turn it off, let it go, or just laugh about it. This will be a result of you becoming an observer of your thoughts — or a listener if you will. You are no longer lost in the sea of words, and you are no longer lost in the darkness of your thoughts where this record plays. Finally, you are able to see that you were scared of this record, believing that what you were listening to was right, when, in fact, it was only repeated long enough to make you believe in it.

Now, your power lies in you — *you* are the observer of your thoughts, and *you* select which ones will make the final cut. You are the director of this film, and some thoughts are like bad actors, in that they can only convince you if you are not knowledgeable in this area — but, since you are the director now, sorry, they won't make it. Your film continues without them.

To improve your mindfulness, take a walk, which helps more than you think. It is like an active meditation. Go on a walk by yourself, and if you can, go hiking in nature. There is nothing better in the world for clearing your mind, getting rid of stale energy, stale thoughts, and sharpening your mindfulness.

Any walk won't do. Make sure you set an intention that you'll have a mindful walk. It could be a brief walk in the park, around your neighbourhood, or in the woods.

Start by noticing how your shoes feel on your feet. Observe the ground under your feet and how it feels walking over it. Slowly transfer your attention from the ground to your surroundings. Notice the people that pass by you, how their faces look. Can you spot their emotions based on their body language?

Observe the architecture, nature, trees, grass, animals, and birds. Don't think, or analyze, simply observe them. Don't try to create a story about the people, merely acknowledge their body language with one word.

Be entirely present during your walk. Be present and aware of every step you take. This mindfulness walk can last for as long as you feel like walking.

CHAPTER 3 – MINDFULNESS

Our mindfulness is affected by many things. We are distracted by millions of things during our day — television, the internet, computers, phones, social media, noise, traffic, and other people.

While practising mindfulness (it does not matter in what form it is — doing nothing, meditation, observation of your thoughts, or walking), you are practising to learn how to stay away from your distractions.

And here I mean mostly about the gadgets that have already taken over us. Yes, we cannot imagine our lives without the internet, texting, sending emails, using, and abusing social media. But if you want to slow your mind down, quit comparing yourself and even soothe the feelings of sadness, and depression, you genuinely need some rest from it all.

I don't know how disciplined you are when it comes to using your phone and social media, but I want you to remember the last time you were not able to use your phone (because the internet was down and you wanted to enjoy it more).

We can all survive without social media. The more we use them, the more addicted we are. And the more we stare at our phones or computers, the more we become passive and get lost in a sea of thoughts that barely serve us.

My suggestion is to give yourself a rest from social media. I know it cannot be done immediately and drastically, but you can always practice. And every time you decide to be mindful and practise mindfulness is the time when your phone shouldn't be in your hand.

Do nothing, relax your eyes, relax your brain from fabricated fake life collected in one photography.

Only in these mindful moments, you'll realize how much time we waste on doing "nothing." This "doing nothing" affects our productivity, memory, and mindfulness, and forces us to compare to others (the first thing you need to stop doing if you want to boost your confidence).

So, to close this chapter, mindfulness is liberating in every meaning of the word, because we learn that every moment passes and that nothing is given forever — neither the bad nor the good moments.

Being mindful will help you learn more about yourself, and will make you aware of the things you do, say, or think. And our thoughts are the only reason why we feel this or that way.

And how is confidence connected to mindfulness? Very simple — the more you are observing your thoughts, the more you are able to detect the good ones from the bad (and limiting) ones. Being mindful about the things, thoughts and people that don't serve you'll help you to let go of them. And when that happens, you get to see a clear picture of yourself. You begin to love what you see and who you are becoming.

CHAPTER 4

Changing Old Beliefs

Chapter four will be all about old beliefs, or core beliefs if you will. We all have them. Some of us are aware of them, while others have no idea they exist. However, these core beliefs make us take actions or restrain us from taking risks or making decisions. They made us believe we are a certain way — good-looking, ugly, complicated, weird, awkward, unintelligent, good at something, and so on.

I pointed out mostly negative traits because the core beliefs that are positive work right for us. You won't see a person who believes he or she is good at something, having second thoughts, fear their decision, or feel inadequate. When the belief is positive, it drives us forward and helps you achieve things.

But what happens when the belief isn't right? What happens when the belief is so old, so deeply rooted in you that you are no longer able to make a difference where it begins and where it ends?

To answer this, you first must look inside yourself. Many people would say that they don't know or cannot see their limiting beliefs. They would say that they are this way or that way, but never, in a million years will they be able to recognize that their thoughts or beliefs, were instilled by someone else or even by themselves.

Old beliefs are something that we have allowed to stay in our heads for a long time, until it was so large and so real, that we were not able to realize that it was not valid.

For example, you might have been an overweight child (like me), and someone said that being fat is bad, or you heard someone making fun of a fat celebrity or saying things like fat people are lazy. It happened so early in your life that you were not even able to know that people (even children) tend to say mean things only because they are frustrated with themselves (or have learned this habit in their early years). Perhaps they heard this from another person (parent, teacher, grandparent).

You are holding on to these thoughts, trying to find what is wrong with you, although you were a happy child that was not burdened with any thoughts about weight whatsoever.

And it begins. You can only see a person that looks ugly, fat, and unattractive. Even if you have extra weight, it does not necessarily mean that you are an ugly man or a woman. But, you give attention to this belief, you feed it with thoughts and overthinking. You feel terrible about yourself, believing that no one could ever love you until you completely transform the way you look.

And then, a relationship occurs, things go well, then it ends, and you connect the ending with this old belief. You believe that your partner did not love you enough, or decided to stop your relationship because you don't look good enough or because you have a few pounds more. In reality, the end of the relationship has nothing to do with this, but your old belief is now loud and does not allow you to listen to any other rational thought. You even see this as a fact.

We have all been there. Limiting beliefs tend to stop us from doing things in life. They are the main reason why we self-sabotage ourselves. The deeper the roots, the more challenging it will be to get rid of the core belief.

But, just because something is challenging, it does not mean that it will be impossible.

The great news is that you are in power to detect and change every limiting belief you have with the belief that serves you, inspires you, and helps you grow in every area of your life.

Some people, as I mentioned in the first chapter, are not ready nor able to recognize or understand their limiting beliefs. They believe that their personality is the way it is. If they have convinced themselves that they are not good at something, are not lovable,

CHAPTER 4 – CHANGING OLD BELIEFS

capable of doing things, are not good people, they will continue living their lives restraining themselves from doing the things they are very much capable of doing.

I have been one of those people who had limiting core beliefs. I was not aware of them entirely, although I knew that my state of mind was quite a mess. I knew that I was not in the right place, and yet I was not doing anything to change it.

As I already mentioned at the beginning, I am dyslexic and was never quite the best at spelling or grammar. It presented such a challenge for me. I was embarrassed away from reading in front of people, and I thought that being dyslexic was a huge setback in many things and in many ways. I was so embarrassed about my writing and so afraid I would misspell, that I used to get my husband to sign all the certifications for courses I ran in my holistic clinic. I've only been signing them myself for a year now, so as I say it takes time.

Although I was never good at spelling, writing, or grammar, I was always good at talking to people. I knew what to do with words when they were coming out of my mouth. However, it took me a long time to recreate my beliefs, to turn them upside down to see my strength. I kept working the same job for eleven years because I was not brave enough to challenge myself to get out of my comfort zone. I was doing mostly factory work, I was spending the more significant part of the day at work, and I was missing my children's early years. It was killing me, and I desperately wanted a change. I decided to change my job, but more importantly, I needed a change in my beliefs, in my future and an upgrade of my knowledge about spirituality.

I know, both from personal experience and the experiences of other people, that you won't start changing your beliefs until you truly and sincerely wish to make a change in your life.

You might want to change your job because it does not pay well, or because it drains your energy, but your limiting belief that you are not good enough for anything else will keep you there for years.

You might want to leave your partner who isn't suitable for you and makes you feel bad about yourself and the things you want, but you have convinced yourself that it is hard to find new love. You believe that you won't be able to go through another new relationship, nor will you ever find someone better.

These are just a few examples of core beliefs. Are they true?

Of course, they are not. And it seems that everyone else can see it, but you. You will only be able to see it when you learn what your limiting beliefs are doing to you.

Sometimes, this step takes a few weeks. Other times, it may take a few years. You will first need to become so fed up with your core beliefs and the way they make you feel so that you can honestly say to yourself, *Things are not working out for me like this anymore.*

Even then, it may be a bit foggy for you.

How can you detect these beliefs?

Usually, we are more capable of noticing a limiting belief in another person. It is because we see the whole picture, and we are able to see their qualities and skills much easier than them. They have willingly put blindfolds over their eyes and act as if they cannot see when all they need to do is remove the blindfold.

However, if someone else does not point out that we have a specific limiting belief, the burden falls to us. It is our job to detect it.

Start by simply writing down your beliefs on things such as career, family, love, your physical appearance, the things you are doing in life, people you are with, and so on.

Do you desperately want to start a creative career, but you come from a family where you all believed (and they taught you) that a job that pays you enough for your bills and food is all you need?

Have you convinced yourself that having a partner (no matter if they are negative or not) is the meaning of life and that being single is a reflection of you?

Perhaps you want to earn more money, but you believe that making money is a tough thing.

CHAPTER 4 – CHANGING OLD BELIEFS

You can extend this writing exercise or method by creating sentences such as:

I cannot leave the job that I hate, because _____.

Leaving this town is impossible, because _____.

Everything that comes after the "because" is your limiting belief. I suggest you write down the exact things you firmly believe keeps you away from the things that you want to do. Don't overthink, don't seek for reasonable things, just write.

And there are your limiting beliefs.

Now that you have discovered them, let's see what makes you think this way.

Maybe you were raised to believe that being single is bad. Or perhaps your parents affected your self-acceptance, convinced you that you have to fit in society by their measures. Probably your friends changed your beliefs somehow — maybe they made you believe that making it in another country or city is mission impossible, and you believed that. Or perhaps you did not believe in yourself enough to go against other people's beliefs to prove to yourself that they were wrong.

Our limiting beliefs can be instilled by TV, films, or even by ourselves, but once we are able to detect them, we have done a great job.

The more challenging part arrives when you decide to change them.

You see, it isn't easy to convince yourself that you were not right when you were feeding your mind with these limiting beliefs. They are so deeply instilled, that now it seems crazy to change them.

We have talked about self-acceptance, setting goals, and mindfulness combined with meditation.

I was so detailed about these things at the beginning because I know they are the powerful keys that will unlock you from this dark place where you keep your record player and let it repeat the same record over and over again.

What Are the Most Efficient Ways to Change Your Limiting Beliefs?

There are many ways that can help you change your limiting beliefs. My first instinct is to tell people that they don't have to see these beliefs as foreign bodies they need to get rid of. If you instill that in your head, you are only breeding another limiting belief, and things might not go smoothly.

Your limiting beliefs (it does not matter how they ended up in your head) can be changed, rather than "destroyed" or removed. You see, when you approach the core belief with the intention to change it, rather than take it out of your mind, you start slow. You start with baby steps, with easiness, and with love.

This love is for yourself and your old ways. Sure, you did not know any better, and you were feeding yourself with beliefs that did not serve you, but it is high time you start acting nice towards you. Don't be negative or mean in this process, solely because of yourself. When things are done by force are usually not bringing good results. In fact, if you decide to do this change by force (or if you choose to "erase" your beliefs), things might not go as you hoped.

So, let's start easy, and here are my suggested steps.

1. Find the core belief. First, you need to detect the core belief before you change it. But, very often, even for people who are convinced they are positive and good, realize that their limiting beliefs are sugar-coated in layers and layers that are making it hard for them to detect them. For example, you might think you are doing great, and there are no limiting beliefs that are stopping you from living your life the way you want to. Sometimes your positive attitude might not be enough, especially if you are not noticing your words. You might be saying negative things to yourself and the people around you, without even being aware of it. I know this sounds a little confusing, but here is the example. Stressful situations, pressure, difficult times can be quite challenging, so remember what you usually say when you find yourself at such a moment. Many people who are not aware of their limiting beliefs and have a great attitude won't catch little phrases such as, "See, I'm not smart enough," or

CHAPTER 4 – CHANGING OLD BELIEFS

"See, I simply cannot do this," or "I knew it, I am not good enough," etc.

These phrases might seem innocent and not threatening at all, but are in fact as dangerous and as damaging as any other negative phrase that people with limiting beliefs say to themselves. If you are not sure whether your core beliefs are hiding behind your positive attitude, notice the words you are saying when things are not going your way.

2. Start observing. Sometimes we don't even have to have negative self-talk or a loud inner critic to feed a limiting belief. This is perhaps an even more dangerous thing because we have decided to shut down the negative thoughts. So how can you know? Start noticing the things around you — see the patterns, notice the people that surround you. Are you entirely content with the places you go, your job, house, friends, partner? Are your relationships with people usually ending fast or they last even though they are not pleasant? Are your friends there for you, or are they typically busy when you call them? Are you able to complete a goal, even if it is something simple?

These patterns will tell more than any thought or phrase you use for self-sabotage. Ask yourself what you think about that situation. and be honest. Your answers should be brief and fast — don't analyze or overthink, just say it.

"That goal was going to fail anyway."

"My friends are only using me when they need me."

"I am unlovable, that's why every relationship fails/I won't leave my partner because he/she is the best I can get."

These possible answers are just an example of limiting beliefs. Even if you don't think this way every day, you allow yourself to be stuck in situations that don't help you grow and live your full potential. Your answers are just the windows that you have now opened and saw how things really are.

You need to ask yourself what you truly want, and what you need to believe in to have the life you desire. When you have the answer to both questions, you have made the first step towards the change.

3. Awareness and mindfulness. We can't go anywhere without this method. It can be painful, challenging, and demanding, but once you realize you are doing it, you'll see how much it will help you. We are all capable of being mindful and aware, although we live in a time where there are so many things that can distract us and take our attention. Awareness comes as the next logical and natural method after you complete method 1 and 2. I don't deny that you can start with awareness first and then apply the first two methods — my suggestion is to start detecting your core beliefs and notice the patterns in your life. Awareness or mindfulness is the most practical method that not only will make you realize that every moment in life matters, but it will help you become an observer of your own thoughts. Being aware means to observe, so, observe your words. Whenever you catch yourself starting your sentences with complaining words, cut yourself immediately. Observe your thoughts and allow them to pass through your mind. See their effect — notice what negative thinking tries to do. It seeks to persist, to stay there, to become a cluster, to become so large that you won't be able to get rid of it.

When you are aware, and when you practice mindfulness, you'll soon become a master of observation. You become more understanding of your old beliefs. The more you observe and the more aware you are of your patterns, why you stick to your core beliefs, and why you allow such behaviour, the more you are going to be able to change them. Awareness becomes your golden ticket, if you will, on your way to the realization that sticking to your limiting beliefs or patterns don't work for you well. Only then you'll be able and willing to change them.

I keep saying that changing core beliefs might be tricky for some people, while for others, it will be done without problems. The more mindful you are, the more you build your awareness, the easier it will be for you to let go of some old thinking patterns. When you are aware, you see it all — you understand and accept your habits of thinking and behaving. You can detect where they came from. As an

CHAPTER 4 – CHANGING OLD BELIEFS

aware person, you know why this was happening, which is why it is much easier for you to change the old belief and to recreate your thoughts.

4. In my first chapter, I told you where I wrote my limiting beliefs on one side of a sheet of paper "as a table" and beliefs that work for my well-being on the other. You can use this method if you want so that you can create a visible contrast. Write all the things that are weighing you down — be brutally honest, don't write kind words. Your old beliefs are not lovely; therefore, you don't have to lie. I know it feels a little bit unpleasant when you have to write them down because suddenly they become so visible "they stir emotions within" you when you look in the sheet.

When you write them down and see all the negativity that was staying in your head, it feels alarming. Write the new beliefs, the ones that work for you that help you grow and become a better person. When you have this "black & white" table, please read it out loud. Some of the old beliefs will feel like total nonsense. You will feel as if though they are entirely fake and that they don't work with you. Nobody wants to read it out loud that they are not good enough, not lovable enough, etc. But, you'll know which of these core beliefs is your challenge, when you write the positive beliefs that should be their total opposite. So, if your old limiting belief is about you being difficult to love, or unable to be in a good relationship when you write that you are lovable and capable of bringing a lot in the table when you are with someone, it might not feel real for you.

Don't worry, this is just your old belief trying to survive. Old beliefs cannot be erased within a day — my suggestion is to start with small steps. Naturally, you cannot jump on the mountain peak when you are at the base. You have to start climbing it, step by step, and you'll sweat, and huff and puff, but you'll make it. Climbing to the summit of the mountain and seeing the entire picture will be your reward. You will have to train your mind to start believing in something else, so it may take time.

If you have convinced yourself that you are not good at something, you are not lovable, or that you cannot get a certain job, you'll have to find mild substitutes for these core beliefs.

RADIATE CONFIDENCE — Sharon Ledwith

Do you think that you are not lovable? Write down all the things you like about yourself. Write the things the people close to you love about you.

Do the same with your other core beliefs. If it feels unrealistic for you to start believing in something new and positive, make it more realistic for you. Let's say you don't think you are capable of getting a new and better job.

Try this belief: "Every day, I change my old belief that I cannot get a new and better job. Every day, my old beliefs are becoming so small and insignificant, that I cannot help myself but believe that I am capable, competent, smart, and suitable enough for the job I desire."

Let this template be a base for any other core belief you find challenging for changing.

5. Educate yourself. You are already doing this by reading these lines. My suggestion is to widen your horizons. Nothing is more helpful than reading books that are going to help you discover more about yourself. Psychology, self-help, spiritualism, mindfulness, just any genre will be of great use. I have done the same — my goal was to improve my spiritual knowledge, and on the way, I realized many things. Reading all of these books helped me understand many things about the way I used to feel. I became aware of mindfulness and how important it is. My understanding of my depression and self-sabotage was crystal clear. It felt nice to be able to understand and accept myself fully.

6. Gratitude. It seems like we cannot go anywhere without gratitude. The thing about being grateful lies in the fact that the more you do it, the more aware you become of the things you have, know, do, and think. Gratitude is just one form of being aware and mindful. When you are giving thanks to the universe, God, or the creator, you are acknowledging the things that make your life easier. You are aware that these things are helping you do your work better. You are aware that your life is more abundant, thanks to the people in it. When you are giving gratitude, don't forget to thank yourself or your mind for being able to detect all the negative thinking patterns. When you are mindful, your mind is finally ready to catch the bad thinking, and

CHAPTER 4 – CHANGING OLD BELIEFS

you, as an observer, know that such thought isn't of any use. Thank yourself for being able to do this.

7. Put your accomplishments on display – If you were raised to be modest and not talk about your achievements with pride, it is time to do something different. I don't say you should brag about the things you have achieved on your social media (although it isn't a bad idea if it makes you feel better). My suggestion is to write down everything you have achieved so far. Whatever feels like an accomplishment, go ahead and write it down. It could be anything from graduation, to starting your own business, traveling with your family, moving out, or ending a negative friendship or a relationship.

Write it down, use photographs or videos from these moments (if you have any) and create an accomplishment board. Look at it every day and thank yourself for going through it, for setting goals and finishing them, for being kind, hardworking, dedicated and smart enough to do all of it. Do you know how many big and small accomplishments you are doing every day? It is time for you to start acknowledging them this way. So, next time, your core belief tries to kick in and attack, look at this list or board, and you'll know that whatever the inner critic is saying isn't valid.

8. Visualization. I love this method because it is fun, does not cost anything, and makes me feel so great afterwards. You can use it for anything from a manifestation of the things you want, to accomplishing your goals, and even in changing your core beliefs. Visualize yourself feeling good — see yourself being able to get rid of the negative thoughts that make you feel like you are not good enough. Visualize these core beliefs as a piece of paper — see yourself crumpling it and making a ball. Visualize throwing this paper ball in a fire, in the bin, in the fire, just anywhere where it will be destroyed and gone forever. Visualize yourself feeling easier, lighter, better.

9. Create a picture of the person you want to be. Without any limiting beliefs, guilt, negative emotions, expectations, or fear of the outcome, visualize or write down what you want to become, achieve and do in your life. Create this vision without being afraid that people will drag you down, without fear that you'll fail. Create it as if though you are writing a fantasy script.

Speaking of this, many people I have talked to, tell me that no matter how glorious this picture is, they are simply unable to believe it nor start working towards its realization. The old beliefs are strong, and practising the methods might seem like you are lying to yourself. Some people will worry and fear that no matter what they want to change, it won't happen, because of many reasons. Creating a picture of the things you want to have and accomplish might be unrealistic when your core beliefs are still loud. This is part of the work you need to do to change them. Your need for a change should be stronger than anything, even your stale beliefs.

Use this method as one of the many you'll work with, but if this particular feels fake, and you constantly find issues with it (you can't believe you could achieve the thing) then you need to accommodate this method. Some people tend to go all or nothing, and they use this big picture they created as a thing that helps them emerge on the surface when the limiting beliefs strike. Others would instead create a picture that isn't going extremely against their limiting beliefs. For example, people who fight their core beliefs and find it hard to believe in the picture they want for themselves tend to create smaller visions of the large image. They create a picture where they can see themselves saying "no" to people, for example.

See what works better for you, what feels right and use it. This method, combined with mindfulness, can help you elevate to a much higher level where you'll be able to start creating beliefs that work well for you.

10. Healthy statements. Did you know that the right affirmations can help you re-wire your brain and change the things you have convinced yourself were true? I left the good statements or affirmations as the cherry on top on purpose. Using these methods works like a miracle. But to make the whole path even more pleasant and to boost your mind with something nice, I suggest you start using affirmations. What we repeat, what we give our focus on becomes our reality.

The more you allow positive thoughts and positive self-talk without complaining to take place, the better you'll feel. If you gave so much time to these old beliefs and let your inner critic repeat these negative thoughts over and over again, then the process is definitely

CHAPTER 4 – CHANGING OLD BELIEFS

possible with the positive thoughts. Affirmations will help you erase all the things that were stopping you from seeing your entire glory and do stuff you firmly believed you were not capable of. So, instead of feeding the "I am not good enough" thought, change it to, "I am good enough, and what other people say is none of my business." You can use, "I am lovable and have relations based on love and respect," instead of something else that would ruin your confidence. Any negative thought or belief has its own positive opposite. Now that you are mindful, you can easily detect this. So, instead of letting your mind go towards negative thinking, redirect it towards the positive.

Conscious and Subconscious Mind and Benefits of Constant Space Repetition

The brain is a mighty organ, and even today, it still surprises us with the way it works. When we learn something new, we have to repeat it a few times so we can memorize it and later, recall this information or knowledge.

For example, when you learn that your friend has a new home address, you have to repeat this address to yourself several times so that you'll remember it. But, the less you use this new information, the greater the likelihood you'll probably forget it. On the other hand, if you use this info, think about it often, and visit your friend there, you *won't* forget it. In fact, you may even learn, additionally, that there's a nice restaurant or two on this same street, a few good clothing shops, etc.

The more you use any piece of information, the more it will stay in your memory. But, on the opposite end, it will fade from your mind the less you use it. Just think of all those people who've moved to another city or country. After several years, they have a hard time remembering the streets of their hometown, they forget their old neighbours, and so on.

This is where spaced repetition comes to hand. This is a learning technique that helps you learn and memorize things with frequent repetition. The more you review certain information, in increasing intervals, the more you'll remember it.

RADIATE CONFIDENCE — Sharon Ledwith

Why am I using this learning method in the chapter for changing your limiting beliefs?

Because it is a perfect example of what you do to your mind when you focus on the same thought over and over again.

In the end, you are convinced in the belief as if it was a fact (which in most cases is not). You continuously repeat this belief in your mind that it becomes so deeply rooted, that when you finally become aware of it, it seems like it is impossible to change it or remove it out of your head.

But, let's use the spaced repetition to benefit. It will help you memorize your affirmations and healthy statements. The more you repeat them, the more you go back to these statements, the more they stay in your mind. And you begin to believe in them, use them and apply them in your everyday life.

How Does the Spaced Repetition Affect Your Conscious and Subconscious Mind?

Your mind is constantly influenced by everything that surrounds you — family, friends, co-workers, TV programmes, car noise, or chatter in the background of the train or of the café.

Now, imagine what happens when you spend most of your time in the same environment. You hang out with the same friends and have the same conversations. Your co-workers continuously talk about the same things, complain, gossip, or tell you what to do. You watch the same programmes (news, shows, commercials).

When you stay in the same environment for a long time, your mind becomes used to it and starts creating a belief system based on the things you hear from the people around you and the things you watch on TV.

Why do you think commercials are so frequent on TV? Their main job is to penetrate your subconscious and make you believe that you need a particular product, and making you believe that you want it very badly.

CHAPTER 4 – CHANGING OLD BELIEFS

Now, imagine what happens when you are a child, and you are in the process of learning new things. Your parents convince you that this is good and that is bad, that two and two are four. They instill their beliefs in you, practically forcing you to believe the same thing as them, although that belief might not be true at all.

As a child, you don't really know much about these things, so you accept them. But, what happens when you grow up and start to build a belief that was instilled in you by your environment?

Our minds are now full of information, memories, knowledge, and it can be a challenge to give extra effort to create new beliefs or detect whether something is real or not. This has nothing to do with you as a person — your mind is simply trying to find ways to slow down and use its energy rationally without having to work extra hours. So, the mind uses previous experiences, which means it will borrow the said belief and will start seeing it as its own.

Let's say a co-worker said that it is almost impossible to get a raise or a promotion in the company where you just started working. This is new information, but your mind picks to take it like realistic because you don't know anything about this new place. If your co-worker says so, then it must be true. And you remain in this company, working hard, hoping for a raise or promotion, but deep down it does not happen because you believe in the thing you heard. So, no matter how much you work, you kind of self-sabotage yourself, by not asking for a raise, or waiting for your boss to see how good of a worker you are. It never happens, and you build your belief even more so. But then, you hear a story of another co-worker who got their raise, or you see others making progress.

So, why has this thing not happened for you yet? It's because you don't believe it could happen to you — you firmly believe that your effort is for nothing, and with the time you quit trying. You go to work, put minimum effort, get your pay rise, and continue living in the magical circle of your old belief, dissatisfaction and wishes for a better future.

Your mind is practically programmed by certain information that is instilled and then seen as necessary enough to stay there long. Your mind considers the information to be essential and lets it stay in your head for a long time.

Some thoughts remain in our focus because we give them attention. It takes a lot of mindfulness work to be aware of which thoughts deserve your attention and which should be dismissed. However, every human being has faced situations where he or she was not able to stop thinking about a certain thing.

The trick is to learn how to choose which thoughts to stay in your focus. It is a real piece of work to be able to focus on the positive thoughts so things will work better for you (pleasant emotions, peace, knowing that positive thoughts can change your reality, just as powerful as negative thoughts can).

To overcome an old belief and to change it with a positive one that works for you can be done with many methods. And sometimes, no matter how much you understand this process, your mind will still choose to focus on the negative things. The thing is we cannot isolate ourselves from people, TV, and live in a quiet environment where our minds won't be overwhelmed with negative energy and people.

Some people are simply packed with negativity and can quickly transfer it to you, even if they are sweet talkers and seem like they don't mean to harm you at all.

So, to become even more aware of the change against negative thoughts and beliefs, you'll have to work frequently. We have the ability to train our minds and constantly challenge them and build them like muscles — the more we talk about the positive things, the more we urge ourselves to change our old beliefs, the better we become at this. But this isn't the easiest job in the world.

As I wrote earlier, our minds tend to go to "energy save mode" to find the easier way, because there is already plenty of work for them.

Kicking out your old beliefs isn't a work you could do once a week or once a month. It is something you need to do, day by day, at any given moment, you become aware of the old belief. You need to want to get rid of this stale belief, more than you are lazy to do it. If you don't go after it, no one else will.

CHAPTER 4 – CHANGING OLD BELIEFS

The more attention you give to your positive thinking and the new beliefs that work for you, the more you'll be able to rewire your mind.

It will take some time, but as I always say, time will pass anyway. Just like your confidence, your mind needs some exercising. It cannot gain "muscles" after only a few minutes of mindfulness and positive thinking.

People ask me how they will know if their old beliefs are gone and whether they have rewired their minds.

When you start feeling better, when you feel that the old beliefs are no longer affecting you when you want to do something, you'll know you are on the right path.

However, our minds can trick us into believing that we succeeded. If you think you have successfully managed to change your old beliefs, but still feel terrible when someone says something, then you still have work to do.

For example, you perhaps are working on your confidence and try to improve your self-image, but when someone mentions things directly about your physical appearance, or the way you look (or used to look) and you still feel vulnerable, there is still a lot of work.

You see, when we are sensitive about certain things in our lives, we tend to take things very personally. Sometimes, we even perceive these things as direct insults. But, can someone really insult you if you don't agree with them? Can someone insult you if the things they say are not real? And most importantly, do you believe in the things people say about you? Do you agree they are real even though they are not?

There is the answer. You have to realize that the belief you hold on to is a fake statement. It does not even have to be directly connected to you. People end up in arguments, trying to defend their opinion, when in fact that isn't even their opinion — they just heard it somewhere, fixed it in their heads, and now believe it's theirs.

When you decide that you are going to break these beliefs and finally see your truth, you are liberating yourself from the never-ending cycle that was not bringing you anything good.

Giving a chance to mindfulness, meditation, affirmations, and observing your thoughts will lead you to places you never knew existed. You will be able to see things that were blurred by the huge belief you thought was right.

You will see that the people around you are not better than you. They are not smarter than you, nor are they doing better than you. Finally, you'll be able to see all the patterns your mind was trying to convince you that you were the only one that was lacking things, or was doing the wrong thing, while everyone else was succeeding.

And one significant discovery that will surprise you is that your feelings are not facts. Feelings are important, and you cannot escape them, no matter what, but whatever you feel at any given moment, it does not mean that it is a fact.

If this was confusing in the past, now it will make sense.

If your friend snapped at you over a little thing and made you feel terrible, it does not mean they hate you. You might end up overthinking and seeking the bad in you (another significant sign of low self-esteem and lack of confidence), but the truth is, even though you felt terrible about the situation, it does not mean their negative emotion and poor choice of words are in fact hatred towards you.

Sometimes people act impulsively, or they had a bad day, or something is bothering them, and they end up arguing with a person that isn't in any way related to their problem. I don't say that you need to look for excuses for people who act negatively to you. You simply need to understand that not every minor inconvenience is because you did something wrong, or because you are not good enough or because someone hates you.

The less you personalize these things, the better you'll feel. And that can only happen as your mind is becoming your friend, not your enemy.

CHAPTER 4 – CHANGING OLD BELIEFS

A mindful person will be able to detach themselves from situations like this. These people will know that it isn't their fault their friend snapped and said a few bad words. Mindful and aware people can easily observe the situation and see that they don't have to engage in this argument at all.

On the other hand, a person who is still trapped in their old beliefs will connect the situation with things that are by no means even close to it. These people will think that their friend finally snapped at them because they are not good enough and not lovable enough. Time will pass, and they will still feel the burden of this inconvenience, believing that the root of the wrong attitude of their friend is entirely and only connected with them. Such thoughts are going to give rise to negative emotions, such as feelings of dissatisfaction with their personality or doubts in themselves ("Am I a good friend?" for instance).

Remind yourself that your emotions are not facts.

When you feel that something isn't right, don't dismiss it. Check your thoughts and what you feel. If there is something that bothers you, talk to someone. If your emotions were caused by a person, have an honest conversation with this person. Maybe the things are not that bad as you think, and in fact, you might have created a scenario in your head believing that it was real.

Allow your emotions to go through you. Your job is to become aware enough to make a difference between the real emotions and those created out of overthinking, worrying, or imagination.

Treating your feelings like facts can cause you a lot of trouble, especially with your beliefs.

In fact, most core beliefs you still feed are nothing but emotions that you misunderstood as facts.

Is it a fact that you are unlovable or maybe you felt that way because you were in a relationship with a toxic person? Perhaps you took this for granted because your parents were always busy, got divorced, or neglected you?

It isn't a fact that you cannot find a better job. It is just a feeling that you held on because you were afraid to challenge yourself. Fear, too, is an emotion.

It took me years of practice to be able to tell the difference between my emotions and the real facts.

It isn't your fault if you are not able to differentiate between them — it is just the way human beings function. I don't think someone can make a difference between these two before they decide to become mindful and work on themselves.

A mind that is asleep cannot know that there is such a thing as a difference between emotions and facts. Only when you dig deep under the surface of your mind and emotions, will you be able to realize that this thing exists.

We are taught, and we live in a world where it is so much more pleasant to live in comfort, even if it is the comfort of our mind. Thinking requires effort, and if you give it, you'll discover many truths about yourself, you would rather never learn.

We choose the feelings over facts because they are more familiar and perhaps not so harsh. And even if they are harsh, we chose them because we want to believe in what our mind serves us.

Sometimes, this can be a coping mechanism that keeps us sane or makes us feel better about ourselves.

I know that the truth is harsh, but we are becoming lazier and I don't mean only about sports and physical activity. We are complacent when it comes to thinking as well. And if we give a little more effort to thinking (call it mindfulness if you want), we will be able to see that most of our emotions have taken a negative form, trying to present themselves as facts.

You don't have to be a psychologist or have a degree from a prestigious school to become mindful and see how your core beliefs take over you in a moment when you were absentminded.

We have all been there. Some of us are still going through this process. The great news is that many people are waking up slowly

CHAPTER 4 – CHANGING OLD BELIEFS

and want to learn what the thing that makes them feel bad and stops them from living their lives is.

Finally, to have certain beliefs is a normal thing, and every human being has them. It is essential to detect the ones that are not serving you.

Imagine your mind as a tree with many branches. The vital branches are providing you with energy, bear fruits, and motivate you to be better, work on your goals and passions. To put it simply — they inspire you.

However, every tree has dry branches that don't have leaves and only drain the energy from the other branches, stem, and roots. They are not allowing young branches to grow and limit you in every way possible. The tree tries to provide these branches with enough juices hoping they will grow, but nothing happens. And while the tree tries to recover these dry and old branches, it leaves the healthy ones behind, not paying attention to them at all.

In the end, the tree becomes dry and begins to decay although there are healthy branches (that in the end, give up the fight, and allow to be taken down with the unhealthy ones).

See your negative and limiting beliefs like these branches. Every time you listen and focus on these beliefs, you are intentionally limiting yourself and your potential because you choose to believe the lies that were instilled in you. You picked the easier way because it was far more comfortable to see your emotions and core belief as valid, rather than check the facts. Focusing on the subjective perceptions and firmly taking them as given facts, does not mean that you have come even close to the real facts.

As an ending to this chapter, I want to point out that our minds need to be under constant maintenance. You should never let the grass overgrow because you won't be able to see where the flowers are, weeds will take over, and it will seem like mission impossible to put the whole garden in order. This is why many people prefer not to go deep into their minds — the place looks like a jungle without any signs that could lead you on the right path.

However, many methods can help you find your way and create order in your head.

The best and most successful method you can use is your own will: Be willing to change, to see where have you lost the track, and to see who or what made you create an entire belief in something that was not true in the first place.

People are often surprised to detect one limiting belief because they are often carefully hidden behind emotions we mistake for facts, or personality traits.

The main reason I added the chapter on limiting beliefs is I know that once you dare to look deep inside yourself and learn the things you knew subconsciously, you'll never want to return to this place again without carrying these methods that will make your mind shine bright.

Remember, the only thing that stands between your goals and you, between you feeling well without needing to judge, seek approval or acceptance is your mind. Either you gain full control over it, or you get lost in the vortex of confusion, limiting beliefs, and overthinking.

CHAPTER 5

The Law of Attraction

You probably wonder why I have dedicated an entire chapter to the law of attraction when this book is about confidence.

When I work with people helping them find their voice, boost their confidence, and improve their spiritualism, I always start with the law of attraction. You see, many people who are not informed don't really know what this means. But that does not mean that if you don't know what it is, that it does not work even as you read these lines.

Everything in life is vibration. For some people, this is a concept that seems a little bit hard to understand, especially when I tell them that they too vibrate.

How do we use our vibration to achieve certain things?

You don't have to believe in the law of attraction, or you may believe in it, but it works either way.

At first, people are confused. They think this is some New Age thing that does not make sense and was only created for the purpose of brainwashing. But let's not be that vain, because the law of attraction has always existed. People in ancient times knew about it, just as the people in the Renaissance knew about it.

The law of attraction is just one of the many universal laws. There is also the law of duality, the law of cause and effect, the law of gender, and so on. (Bob Proctor talks about these laws in his teachings.)

The law of attraction suggests that any human being on this planet can have whatever they desire, as long as they put their focus on it. No matter your age, gender, religion, nationality, you can do this.

Have you found yourself noticing how things are always going the hard way for you? You always had to work super hard for your success (at school, work, in relationships). All the things you wanted to have or achieve were always happening to other people, or no matter how hard you worked for them, they somehow were never in the cards for you.

Have you noticed that whenever you are in the supermarket and try to finish your shopping faster, the moment you head to the cashier, ten other people were running in front of you? Or that the traffic lights on the streets are always red? Or that it seemed like you were ending up always having the most difficult questions on your exams, because, unlike you, others were passing the whole thing effortlessly and without problems? Or, perhaps you always attract people who are dishonest, mean, envious, or toxic (partners, friends, or co-workers).

Whatever we give our attention to, whichever thoughts we've decided to hold on to, will take away our focus. Choosing, whether consciously or unconsciously, to focus on a certain thing, we are going to attract it.

I know it may sound unrealistic, but the more you worry about and overthink something, the more you feel bad about it, and you spend hours and hours checking every possible scenario. In the end, you end up having a bad time, feel terrible (moody, depressed, without energy), and you attract unpleasant people and situations.

Your vibration is on a lower level where it easily attracts things that don't work for you.

To make this even more understandable, let me give you an example.

When I was stuck in my old job, all I could think of was that I disliked going there. My focus was on negative emotions. I woke up and went to bed feeling bad for not having enough courage to quit my job. I felt like I was not giving my best as a parent because I was missing the mornings with my children, which was something I wanted. I felt

CHAPTER 5 – THE LAW OF ATTRACTION

like the job was consuming me in every meaning of the word. So, instead of being a happy mother of two young children and enjoying my family life, I was bitter, focused on the things I lacked, on my negative emotions and I felt like I was not able to see the exit out of the negative cycle.

When you give attention to the thoughts that don't work for you, they grow stronger and have stronger roots. You are not able to see the big picture, and all you can do is keep your focus on the negativity. It seems like there is nothing else to think but the things you hate, dislike, lack, or believe will happen (especially the negative ones).

Sometimes, it takes an external factor to point out things for you, because you are not able to remove your focus from the things you have willingly put there.

To me, it happened after I read *The Secret*. It was the most eye-opening reading experience for me, because, not only did it teach me the things I believed I did not know, but it actually reminded me of everything I knew intuitively.

People often ask me for proof that the law of attraction works. They are eager to tell me there is much proof that it does not work at all.

I always say the things you focus on are the things that will keep appearing in your life. So, you decided to believe or look for flaws or for anything that will prove to you that the law of attraction does not work and the universe is giving you that — it shows you ways that what you believe is right.

The law of attraction is used for manifesting things such as money, houses, cars, relationships, just anything. And when people who want to prove that it does not work, are focused on the lack, they get what they put their attention to. If you focus on the things you don't have, you'll continue not having them. If you shift your focus on the things you have, you'll change your entire way of living. You will start witnessing the manifestation of your wishes.

When I was focused on not seeing a way to quit my job, I was trapped in my own circle of negative thinking. I was focused on the fear of leaving the old job and focusing on the things I wanted to do, which are the things I do today.

When you focus and firmly believe that you cannot afford something the universe is giving you more of that.

But, when you decide to change your thoughts and start seeing opportunities, when you begin to see the good in you, and firmly believe that you'll make it, the universe is going to start responding to your focus.

People who try to prove to themselves that the law of attraction isn't working (whether consciously or unconsciously) will use the tools and then will focus on the absence of the manifestation or will be anxious, unable to let go of the expectations. Naturally, they won't receive what they wished for.

I am not judging these people. Part of the disbelief lies in the old beliefs such as "no good things come fast," "hard work is the only thing you need to do," or "nothing good happens to honest people," "you can't expect someone else to serve you things, if you don't work for them," and the like.

These beliefs don't sound entirely crazy. On the contrary, they make sense. But, if you firmly believe in them and then someone tells you that if you practice the methods of the law of attraction, all you need to do is wish for a thing and then wait for it, then naturally things might not go as smoothly.

The law of attraction isn't about you wishing for a million dollars and then waiting to get it. This isn't how it works, especially not when you firmly believe that you definitely cannot get that much money overnight.

Let's start with something not as big as a million dollars. Big goals tend to scare people, and they break their vibration by being "logical." They think that it's impossible to gain money (even as little as one hundred dollars out of the blue). They tend to think of the impossibilities, as opposed to the possibilities, and they get what they focused on.

CHAPTER 5 — THE LAW OF ATTRACTION

Now, let's say you wished for a little more money to flow in your direction. You don't know how this will happen, but you visualize how great it would be if you get some unexpected money, without working for it. You like the idea, you think of the ways you'll spend the money, how great it would feel. You feel fantastic just by thinking of this. Your visualization is finished, and you let it go, without giving it additional thinking. You simply forget about it.

The universe has got your wish, focus, or vibration. Unburdened as to whether you'll get this extra money or not, you continue with your day, and on your way back home you pass by the grocery store and see they sell lottery tickets and you decide to buy one. Without any grand hope, you do win extra cash, without working for it, and without even thinking that you could win it this way.

This is the way the law of attraction works. It does not serve you a bag full of money in front of your doorstep, but it guides you on paths where you'll be able to find the things you put your focus on and then simply take action.

On the other hand, when a person who isn't so sure about the law of attraction is wishing for some extra money but isn't a firm believer, they will try to find ways to prove that the law of attraction does not work. This person will think of ways they could get money, will count the days and months, and they will think how fast, and how much will they gain. But in the end, they will be so focused on the fact that people just don't get money out of the blue that they will, thus, end up empty-handed. Their focus was on the *lack* — in their heads, there are no ways they can get extra money. They believe that money comes only if you work really hard for it. They might have seen the lottery option, but they crossed it off because they don't think it could happen to them. And just like that, instead of simply enjoying their visualization and letting it flow naturally, instead of not allowing themselves to worry about inhibiting thoughts such as the "how" and the "when" of the thing they wish to manifest, they've then gotten what they've focused on — zero ways of gaining money.

Whatever you believe is true. Nobody can convince you that this thing works if you decided to believe that it doesn't. You will continue seeing people enjoying the good things, wondering what they are doing differently than you when you put so much effort, and you stress about your work, multitask several jobs, and still lack the things you want to have.

When I decided to wake up and learn more about these things, my main goal was to become more spiritual and so I read as many books as possible. My knowledge about the law of attraction was not abundant, but my desire for it was intense, and my vision drove me forward.

My wish was to quit the job and start doing something that would make me feel happy and content. I didn't quite know what I wanted to do at the beginning, but I knew that I wanted to speak to people and help them do better. As I was reading hungrily about the law of attraction and what our minds are capable of doing, I was becoming more and more aware of what I want to work.

The best thing I was doing (besides educating myself and staying engaged doing stuff I like) was my complete relaxation without bothering myself with dates and times. I did not think about how long it would take me to decide to leave my job, finally, or how long it would take me to become what I am today. I only enjoyed the journey. I was visualizing, reading, and I worked on my mindfulness and self-acceptance, and things then started aligning.

When you are raising your vibration, things tend to work out for you. It means you are aligned. You begin by seeing the same numbers everywhere, you see signs related to the things you want to do, meet people that will help you learn something new, or help you get a step closer, even though you did not ask them for any help.

You are aligned with the universe, and it sends you signs. And now that your focus is on the right track you begin to notice things.

I can continue writing about the law of attraction, but I believe things will be brighter if I describe how the process goes step by step.

• Step 1 – Many people wonder why they don't get what they want, without even knowing that they have not precisely identified their goal or wish. They say they want things such as money, love, happiness, and they never give any more details. The universe loves details. It is essential to be specific about what you want. Identify your wish and be specific about it, even if it is something as small as

CHAPTER 5 — THE LAW OF ATTRACTION

catching all green lights when driving. In fact, there are no small or big wishes. The universe does not see it this way. It simply responds to your vibrations and feelings. So, the more detailed you are when you visualize, the better. Remember, when you create your vision, you need to focus on how this visualization makes you feel. People often ask me why this does not work for them when they clearly wished for something, and I always ask, "How did you create your wish?"

When you are identifying your desire, be mindful of your words. For instance, if you say, "I don't want to be late for work again," the Universe "hears" the words "late" and "again." You are starting your desire on the wrong side, just by focusing on the negative thing. Instead, try and create your desire like this: "I would love to arrive on time/catch every green light on my way to work." So, instantly, you are creating a positive attitude. I am offering this simple wish as an example.

Naturally, you can identify your wish with your own words, just make sure you focus on the way which won't send negative vibrations. Also, it is essential to feel great during your visualization. Firmly believe that this will happen for you, without fear. Once you have identified your desire, visualize it — see yourself living this goal or wish. Be detailed. Did you wish for a new car? See yourself driving it. Was your wish about a new loving partner? Visualize how loved and safe you feel next to this person.

• Step 2 – Once you've created your desire and had visualizations about it, it is time to start working on other things, such as your vibration. You vibrate at all times, and depending on your vibration you attract people, situations, and things into your life. Notice that when you are negative, and in a bad mood, you meet people who are similar to you — you tend to attract people who argue, complain, or criticize. On the other hand, when your vibration is on a higher level, you meet people that are pleasant, helpful, and nice.

The same goes for when you are trying to manifest something. Lower vibration tends to create negative feelings, doubt, self-doubt, low confidence, inability to accept yourself and others, and so on. But how do you raise your vibration? There are many methods you can use to do this, and one of my favourites is meditation. Meditation is the purest form of cleansing your mind of the stale energy that your thoughts and old beliefs are creating. Also, it is a beautiful way that will help you calm your body, detect the places where you hold your stress (jaw, core, shoulders), and learn how to breathe. With meditation, you are not only raising your vibration, but you are also learning how to observe your thoughts, which leads to better mindfulness.

Another method that will help you raise your vibration is eliminating your old beliefs, build your confidence, and shut your inner critic. To do that, besides mindfulness and meditation, I suggest you start using affirmations. It may seem that these healthy statements are only words, but when you continuously repeat them you allow your brain to memorize them and just like with any memory, the more you use it, the more you return to it, the more it stays in your mind. And as I already said, fake it till you make it — repeat your affirmations till you realize that they have slowly but surely helped you change your old beliefs.

• Step 3 – You have stated your wish to the universe. Now it is time to let it go. The universe knows what you want, and it will align with you to help you manifest it. It is absolutely none of your business how or when you'll manifest your wish. You wished for it, you firmly believe it will happen, and then close that chapter. Your only business is to stay focused on the things you want to achieve, work towards their realization, but without burdening yourself with the outcome. Many people make a mistake by expecting the result, counting days, being anxious and nervous whether their wish will come true or not. This is where they are lowering their vibration. They worry a lot, and worry is a negative emotion. It creates a cluster of thoughts that are guiding you to imagining all sorts of outcomes that may or may not happen. You worry, and you feed yourself with negative thoughts and stress. And during your process of manifestation is important to feel good. These things are not going to help you align with your wish.

Instead, to be aligned to manifest your extra money, you worry, and the universe sends you more of that. Whatever you put your focus on, you'll get more. If it is a worry of how you'll get more money, it will serve you even more worrying — you'll meet people who will

CHAPTER 5 – THE LAW OF ATTRACTION

complain about not having money, you might even lose some money, find higher prices in the shops. Most importantly, you'll only postpone the manifestation and will convince yourself that the law of attraction does not work. So, let it go. You had your visualization, you sent your wish to the universe, and now it's time to have fun. You need to feel amazing even if this wish does not come true. Why? Because your happiness and good feelings don't depend on the wish and its manifestation. And that is the key. If the wish comes true, that is great, but if it doesn't, that is great also. Of course, you need to take action, but you must never bother yourself with the outcome. Let it all go and have fun.

• Step 4 – Allowance is another thing that many people don't know they need to do when wishing for something. Do you know that most people wish for things, but subconsciously they are not allowing them to happen? This is often happening because of our limiting beliefs — people simply don't believe they deserve to have a lot of money, a new car, a great partner, and so on. Yes, we all wish for these things, but are we allowing them to happen? To allow it to happen means to believe that it is possible. When you allow, you are ready and open to receive. It means when you see an opportunity that could lead you to the manifestation of your wish, you accept it. You let go of your resistance, and you simply go with the flow — you allow the universe to serve you what is best for you.

• Step 5 – Gratitude is one of the proven ways that are not only helping you become more aware of the things and people around you, but also help you become mindful and more appreciative. It is also one of the top five crucial steps that are working miracles when you have granted a wish and work on its manifestation. Be honest about it. Give gratitude from the bottom of your heart for every person in your life. Give gratitude for every little and big thing you have achieved, bought, got, or found. It doesn't matter who you are giving this gratitude to, Universe, God, creator, your parents, yourself, your friends. It is essential to really feel that you are fortunate to have these things and people in your life. This way, you are reminding yourself of your blessings while you are open to receiving more. Create a habit to give gratitude every day and see what happens within a month — you'll completely change your way of thinking. You will be mindful and aware of everything you have and the people that surround you. You will start cherishing even the moments you were not aware of before. Use a gratitude diary or simply think of the things and people you are grateful for every day before bed and every morning when you wake up.

Use the Law of Attraction to Boost Your Confidence, Accept Yourself, and Improve Your Mental State

The law of attraction can be used for literally anything you want to manifest, and your confidence and general mental state are not exceptions.

Once you decide to use the methods of the law of attraction, you need to define which parts of your mental state you want to change.

Perhaps you feel inadequate? Maybe you are a shy person who has a difficult time to express an opinion. Perhaps saying no to people is hard for you. You rarely stand for yourself because you fear that people won't like you.

These are just a few of the signs of weak confidence. People whose confidence needs some polishing usually are not prone to speak up or to speak their minds. They feel that they need to explain their choices and decisions to others, believing that anything they do needs to be approved by others. Also, with signs of low confidence and inability to accept oneself, such as continually apologizing for literally anything, these people tend to speak negatively about themselves and complain often. They don't believe that their opinion matters, have low expectations of themselves, and always worry whether they have said the right thing.

Your level of confidence isn't something for which you should blame yourself. It happens to many people, and thousands of people as you read these lines are trying to improve how they present to the world.

Remember, you are not born with low self-confidence, nor it is your fault that you feel a certain way. Your confidence and the way you see yourselves can weaken if you were bullied or had other negative events impact your life. Sometimes frustrated people would want to make you feel the same way. Many children are raised by parents

CHAPTER 5 — THE LAW OF ATTRACTION

who don't know how to boost their confidence, ending unknowingly making it worse.

However, the good news is that you can do something about it. What I love about the law of attraction is that it can help anyone in their progress. It can help you realize where are your weak spots and what caused them. You can become aware of the things you want to change and improve and finally, get to work and feel better about yourself.

Use the method of visualization to see yourself becoming the person you want to be. See yourself walking confidently as if you have won an award. Visualize how you say no to people when you don't want to do something. Stay in this vision — see every detail, feel the emotion.

I often tell people that they need to be very specific about their wishes and visualization. You need to create a whole story. For instance, I saw myself surrounded by people, talking to them, explaining the things I am writing now.

I was feeling their energies, the way they were looking and smiling at me. This vision was making me feel so happy that I was often shedding tears of joy when I was visualizing myself doing the work I am doing today.

Be free to visualize any situation. After all, this is happening in your head, so why would you restrict yourself and refrain from creating a vision of your perfect self? I admit I had challenges with my own visualizations at the beginning. Whenever I would start visualizing by picturing myself successfully making speeches in front of people, for instance, my inner critic would interrupt it. It was as if my unconscious self was reminding me that this is just a lie, a daydream that might not happen. This inner critic was not so loud. perhaps, but it was there, making me feel as if I was lying to myself.

This is a natural thing. It may happen if you are new to visualizing things or if you still have doubts about the law of attraction.

This is why my suggestion is to let go of any expectations. Instead, remember that you are here now, working on your visualization and that nothing else matters. You visualize because you want to feel better, because it is fun and because it is one of the methods or steps that will take you closer to your goal. If it happens, fine, if not, you'll live.

Visualize situations where you are feeling good about yourself. It could be anything from achieving your goal, buying a new car, traveling to your dream destination, finding your dream partner, and so on.

Once your visualization is over (it can take as little as seventeen seconds to kick in and send your desire to the universe), it's time to relax and let go. You did your job. Your wish is noted, the universe felt your vibration, and now it is time for you to relax.

I know it can be a bit tricky to do this when your wish is to improve your self-confidence and self-acceptance because it all depends on you. But there are ways that will help you do it, even when you let go of your intention and expect the outcome.

This is when you need to boost yourself with meditations and affirmations.

There are endless options for guided meditations online. Pick something related to confidence, improving your self-image, accepting yourself, or becoming the best version of yourself.

Creating a habit to meditate will make you relax. Give yourself a chance and be open to this experience. Just listen to the voice of the narrator and follow their instructions. Dedicate this time to yourself without worrying about others. This meditation time is *your* time, even if it lasts only for ten or fifteen minutes.

Even if you don't have a clear picture of where you want to start with your mental state, regular meditations will help you realize this better.

Meditations (especially if you give mindfulness meditations a try), will improve your observance. You will be able to see where your attention goes. Why do you feel more comfortable giving your focus to worrying thoughts, or self-criticism, instead of positive thinking and self-acceptance?

CHAPTER 5 – THE LAW OF ATTRACTION

What makes us focus on the bad far easier than the good? It seems that we are taught to believe that the good rarely happens, while on guard for the negative situations somewhere near us.

Work on your mindfulness so you can become aware of your thoughts. Find your old beliefs and try to detect when, how, and by whom they were instilled in you.

When you are aware, it will be easier for you to notice negative thoughts. You will be able to cut your complaining words, accept a compliment and accept your wishes, achievements, choices, and decisions as valuable.

At this point, when you are willing to change something about your confidence and self-acceptance, you are already aware that you need to use some boosters. And your boosters come in the form of meditations, positive thinking, change of focus, affirmations, and self-love.

My suggestion is to create your own affirmations or healthy statements. I find it easier to connect with my own personal affirmations, but you can always use any of the affirmations you can find online.

I created my affirmations by creating a contrast list of all the things I did not like about myself, combined with my limiting beliefs.

For every negative self-talk, I had prepared three affirmations.

For example, when I started working on myself there were times when I would have thought that I will never be able to find a job that inspires me or makes me feel happy. My mind was trying to revive the limiting beliefs. Fear was producing worries that I might not be successful, who would come to my clinic because I was afraid of challenging myself. My brain (already mildly rewired) would have warned me with a new and positive thought. I would have either thought or written down some boosting and healthy statement.

Positive statements were my weapon.

For example: "I am such an excellent speaker, and I understand people, I am going to make it in this area. Just trust the process and the timing of your life, Sharon."

Adjust your affirmations to the situation of your life. Use words that are going to inspire you. It is essential to create sentences that are not hiding cynicism or doubt.

For example, there is a difference between these two sentences:

"Money is energy, and there is more than enough for everyone."

"I don't ever want to be without money again."

Can you spot the difference? The first one is relaxed, it does not create any limitations and allows you to relax because you don't have to be in any race or competition to earn your money.

The second one is already setting the negative tone, making you feel anxious, remembering all the times when you lacked money. It makes you feel irritated by the thought, and you are already thinking of possible future times when you might end up without money.

The same goes for your confidence.

Create affirmations that will make you feel good. These words need to stick with you and lift you even when your limiting beliefs are trying their best to stay with you.

Your vibration is everything, so working to raise it a little higher will help you more than you think.

As you work on building up your confidence, you are helping yourself achieve just anything you want. When your confidence is stronger, you don't doubt your ideas, goals, decisions, or opinions.

You just trust them and believe they are valuable because you no longer feel like other people have it better.

In fact, you no longer will have the need to compare yourself with others or see them as the only ideal you need to keep up with.

The law of attraction and its method will help you remove your blockages and see yourself for who you really are.

I know that it feels scary when you see confident and successful people, and your fear begins to kick in. You start to worry about how

CHAPTER 5 — THE LAW OF ATTRACTION

long it will take for you, what sort of milestones you need to pass, how you will make it, and what it takes to be so effortlessly confident and to believe in yourself.

You see, a successful person did not come to this world with success. They simply had a clear desire and vision of what they wanted to do in their life, and they worked towards it. When I say work, I don't only mean physical work — I mean studying, learning, improving their mindset, working on becoming their ideal selves.

All those successful athletes were not born skilled or fast, nor with muscles. They worked for it, but above all, they did not give up on building on their confidence. They accepted who they were, knew their qualities, and decided to become their best version.

You are nothing different than those successful people. You too have your confidence, and all it takes is your choice to work on its improvement.

Start believing in your potential. We all have potential, no matter what you may think. Believe in it as an endless source. You have to challenge yourself and see what you are capable of doing.

Even if you spent years convincing yourself that you did not know how or you were not good enough, you can still improve your mindset.

Confidence will attract success. When you challenge yourself to get out of the comfort zone, seek a new job, start your own business, call this person you like, or even go alone to dinner, you are creating new conditions.

You felt confident to do something that was scaring you off, and then you succeeded. Now, this wonderful feeling drives you forward, and you enjoy your time. Confidence attracts other confident people because like attracts like. When you surround yourself with confident people who know who they are, accept themselves and others, you'll see that not everything is so bad. You will quickly start to notice the great things about yourself, and new opportunities will arrive for you.

Believe in yourself and that you can do anything. I know it seems easier said than done. Take small risks, take a bigger risk, just challenge yourself. Remember, you are not doing this, so other people will say how great and successful you are.

You are doing this because you are working on proving yourself that you are good enough, brave, smart and confident enough to do a thing that will lead you towards the life you want to live. You are doing something that leads you to become the person you always wanted to become.

When you see that you are capable of doing things and you start living your success, you'll begin to expect good things. If in the past you were obsessing over adverse outcomes and all things that could go wrong, now you'll notice that you are expecting good outcomes.

With the law of attraction, you are helping your brain change its focus. Use the method of mindfulness, then, and make the law of attraction even stronger. Be mindful of your thoughts and replace them with affirmations when you notice they turn into self-criticism or worries. Shift the spotlight of your attention from everything you are not, to everything you are. This won't only help you start accepting yourself and be who you are, but you'll also begin to attract things and people who compliment your best talents and features.

Expecting the good out of every situation is another law of attraction method. Use it to improve your life, but also your confidence, your worrying habits, and your anxiety.

Instead of imagining negative outcomes, imagine how things will go as everything falls in place. Stick to this vision and expect it. Be open to it, and be willing to receive it.

Even when your mind will give its best to convince you that you are wrong, be firm in your determination to expect the best. There will be resistance, but see this as a regular thing that must happen because your old beliefs struggle to remain where they are now.

When you notice that resistance is affecting you, fight back with reading more successful stories. Start watching films or videos with

CHAPTER 5 — THE LAW OF ATTRACTION

proof that the law of attraction works and helped millions of people become better, successful, accept themselves and live their dreams.

Finally, be persistent when it comes to accepting yourself. This is so simple, yet so complicated for many people. Nobody else will accept you if you don't accept yourself first. Yes, you have flaws, good and bad sides, but who does not have them?

Use your affirmations in this process of acceptance. Create statements about your uniqueness, your talents, good traits, and looks. You are you, and no other human is exactly like you. If you have spent half of your lifetime criticizing yourself and using negative self-talk, now it is high time for you to start doing the total opposite. Talk nicely to yourself. Whenever you practice mindfulness say your favorite statements to yourself. Do this as often as it is necessary for you to believe in that.

And what is more important, to allow the best outcome to happen, accept it and believe that you deserve it. Believe that you deserve to feel happy, content, confident, and loved. Believe it not because I say so, or because you read about it online or watch videos, but because you truly feel that feeling good about yourself is the only natural state for you.

Manifestation

Most people find manifestation to be the most significant challenge once they start practising the law of attraction. People seem eager to take all the steps (use the methods such as meditation, affirmations, visualization, changing their beliefs) and then they suddenly go flat when it comes to manifesting things.

This often happens because people are obsessed with the outcome, without knowing that they are hurting the process with worries, questions, self-doubt, disbelief, and finally, with resistance.

When you work on manifesting your desires, you first need to learn the biggest lesson of them all — letting go and allowing it to happen.

It may sound contradictory, but let me explain.

When you have declared your wish, and you want it to happen fast, you need to be sure whether this wish is something that you truly and honestly want. Many people want to manifest a relationship because they see that everyone else around them is settled. They want a partner because everyone else does. They see the relationship as a logical timeline as they grow older. People think that a relationship will magically make them happy and content, will erase all their negative self-talk, will improve their confidence, and, finally, will make them better people.

They firmly believe that all of this will happen once they find the right person. And what happens? They still have resistance towards the right person or a relationship in general and end up waiting and worrying about their manifestation. They feel bad, sad, depressed, and believe that either something is wrong with them or the law of attraction does not work.

You see, the universe has its own ways, and if you are not feeling good while visualizing or honestly wishing for a healthy relationship, it won't respond. Your focus is still on things such as "when" or "why." You still haven't switched your focus to see the great things about yourself, learn and accept yourself, and be comfortable by yourself. Even if you are not aware of it, a relationship might not be the thing you need at that moment. You are visualizing and using all the methods, but your vibration is still low.

When you try to manifest things, you need to be honest with yourself and your wishes. And to be honest with yourself, you truly need to look deeper inside your feelings, beliefs, and thoughts. This is where meditation will be of great use.

You cannot manifest anything if there is no energy behind it. You can spend hours, days, and weeks visualizing, but if there is no energy or any emotion, nothing will happen. It means you either don't need the thing you want to manifest, or you are just not investing yourself enough.

Another thing why your manifestation isn't happening yet is because you still haven't learned how to work on your affirmations and you haven't changed your general state of mind.

CHAPTER 5 – THE LAW OF ATTRACTION

Let's say you truly want a good relationship, you visualize, use affirmations and meditations, but you keep saying and thinking things such as "I hate being single." You cannot find or manifest this person (or anything you want to have) as long as your attitude is negative. You are practising the law of attraction, but you haven't had fully understood it.

Your visualizations may be the best, and your affirmations can be powerful, but you still have plenty of work to do with your mind. It won't happen overnight, remember that.

Next time when you wonder why you are still not manifesting the thing or person you wanted, just observe what you say and what you think. Especially be careful about the thoughts that pass through your head without you being mindful about them.

You cannot expect to manifest anything if you continuously keep thinking and talking about the thing you don't want to manifest.

People who take this whole thing for granted will struggle to manifest anything that isn't aligned with their beliefs. You cannot expect to become a millionaire when you firmly believe that it is impossible for you for various reasons. You are convinced that only people who are born rich can become richer or that it simply cannot happen to you. You cannot see how you can earn a lot of money, and that kills your manifestation.

So how do you expect to land a better paying job or win the lottery when your core belief is the total opposite of your desire? It will never happen, because every time you visualize, wish, and hope deep down, even if you are not conscious about it, you don't believe that it could happen to you.

Your core beliefs need to change, and no one else will do it for you.

Your wish needs to be precisely defined and detailed. If your desire to get a pay rise is expressed as "I want money" or "I want a car," things will go flat. You are not working on creating a detailed visualization, so the manifestation won't happen any time soon.

Your desire has to be so strong, and you need to believe firmly in it. This wish of yours should be as powerful and stir something inside you. The thing you want to manifest should be a thing you know will occur in your life. No doubts, fear, or worry should be even nearly as strong as your desire.

People ask me why they witness the thing they wished for in their surroundings, but it has not manifested in their lives yet. When you start observing your desire around you (you spot the car you want, or see happy couples around you, for example) don't be envious. Be satisfied that you see these things, in that the universe is showing you that your desire is very much possible.

Instead of envying these people and hating them because they have what you lack, thank the universe for presenting your wish in front of your eyes. Envy can be a disturbing emotion while you work on your manifestation because it shifts your focus to the things you lack.

Keep the faith and most importantly, let it go. People are confused with the "let go" part when I tell them that they need to keep their focus on their wish, but also let it go.

Keeping your focus on the wish means that you are working to improve your state of mind, become mindful about where your thoughts go when things are not going smooth. Also, it means that you work towards manifesting your things. But, you are not obsessing about the outcome. Your job is to be in a good place and to feel good about it. What you shouldn't do is worry about the ways and time of manifestation. This is the let go part. You go on with your day, do your things, but half a minute before sleep is more than enough to feel excited about the wish you made. That is all.

The law of attraction works whether we believe in it or not, whether we practice it consciously or unconsciously.

You can pick any of the methods I offered to test whether it works or not, but either way, what you focus on will keep appearing in your life.

When you learn that only a switch in your focus can be the key to start living a new life, you learn everything.

CHAPTER 5 – THE LAW OF ATTRACTION

There is no magic or particular spell that will speed up the manifestation to work. The law of attraction and the universe simply respond to your vibration.

When you feel inadequate, unimportant, you see yourself as a victim, and you pity yourself, you attract people with the same state of mind, or worse, people who see you that way.

On the other hand, when you decide to change something about the way you think, feel, and how you see yourself, your life changes as well.

I did not master this whole thing in one day. My goal was to improve myself by reading more about these topics, and on my way, I detected all my emotional wounds and realized where I needed to work more so I could heal.

Sometimes, reading about these things work like pouring oil into your car — it will help you move from the place you were standing for so long.

It all comes down to the thing that to improve your thoughts, confidence, and start accepting yourself, you'll first have to realize that no one else will do it for you.

We all live in our heads, and our reality only exists in our mind. In order to change it and witness better things, both externally and internally, we first must clean all the mess that lies in our minds. Every little piece of negativity in the form of core beliefs, criticism, frustration, or just negative self-talk must go.

Everything you have and live today was once an idea in your head. Even the bad things you live today were once just a little thought that managed to steal your focus. This thought grew large and you started manifesting it in various forms such as negative relationships or friendships, difficulties at school or work, depression, complaining, and inability to accept yourself.

Now that you know that everything is in your hands and that your mind is powerful to switch from one point to another, you are free and capable to start this change.

In the end, you can convince yourself in just about anything, if you repeat the right things enough times in your mind and if you use the good words instead of the complaints.

When you relax, and you let go of the worries and the timing of when things need to happen for you, you continue with the flow.

You are unique, and it is high time you start appreciating that. You can do whatever you set your mind to. Start talking kindly to yourself, give yourself compliments, and thank yourself when you do something right.

I like comparing thoughts with suggested videos on YouTube — the more you switch to the positive ones, the more your mind will "suggest" similar thoughts. You are in control to pick the good ones.

Dismiss the negative ones that don't serve you. Just like on YouTube, all it takes for you is to "click" the option "I am not interested in" when a negative thought appears.

CHAPTER 6

Meditation

I was mentioning the magnificent effects of meditation for five chapters, and now I am finally giving it the spotlight it deserves.

Meditation is a practice in which you let yourself be calm physically while you allow your focus to go to a particular thing. Your focus can go to a mantra, breathing, part of your body, or simply the voice of the narrator (if you are following a guided meditation).

In some languages, such as the Indian, meditation means training of your mind. It sounds a bit strict, but in a way, it is training. You are training your mind to calm down, become still, manage to keep its focus on one thing only. You allow the never-ending stream of thoughts to work without disturbing your focus.

I like to explain meditation as a personal dedication. I see it as divine help that allows me to go deeper into my mind and spirit. Sure, it is a training of the mind, and it is one of the best disciplines you could follow because of the benefits you'll gain.

To meditate means to clear your mind of all the debris it collected during the day. Our mind produces about sixty to seventy thousand thoughts per day. That is a huge number, and no person could be entirely aware of every single thought that passes through their head. This is why the thoughts that go unnoticed can do real damage to our mental state.

I have heard various excuses from people who have resistance against meditation, and every single one of them turned out to be wrong, once these people started meditating.

One of the most popular core beliefs is that meditation can be done only by meditation gurus or yogis. The truth is, you can be a young child and still be able to meditate successfully.

Another excuse that I often hear is the inability to stay calm because people believe they are too temperament for something so "boring" like meditating. Others think that it isn't natural for a human being to stay still for twenty minutes or so. Or, that meditation makes them nervous or anxious.

Your temperament has nothing to do with your ability to meditate. You can be vivid, talkative, and bubbly extrovert who cannot imagine your life without action. Still, that does not mean you won't be able to stop for a little while and allow your mind to calm.

When you are a beginner, it is beyond natural to think that you cannot do this, because you don't know how to do it. Your mind faces something new, and this new thing requires a dedication of the focus on one thing, while your thoughts are fighting to steal the attention.

It is normal to feel like you are doing things wrong, but there is no such thing as wrongdoing while meditating.

For beginners, I always recommend simpler and shorter meditations or even guided meditations.

Another thing I always mention is that meditation isn't entirely reserved for people who are under stress, suffer from depression, or have issues with anxiety. You can have your life under control and be a successful person with great confidence, and still meditate regularly.

Meditation is recommended when you feel anxious, stressed, if you worry too much or if you feel depressed. But it is a free cure for all sorts of mental burdens, as well as physical relaxation and calm sleep.

All you need is fifteen minutes to half an hour per day so you can bring balance to your life. Everyday meditation will significantly lower your stress, will improve your focus and will make you more aware and mindful of your thoughts, of the present moment, of your words and actions.

CHAPTER 6 – MEDITATION

The western countries were not familiar with meditation for a long time, and meditation became popular in the past decades. In India, on the other hand, meditation was considered a divine process for centuries and millennia.

When you decide to meditate, you choose to step into a deeper consciousness. You become mindful and raise your awareness, become spiritual, and awaken your creativity, improve your focus, intuition, and relax.

If you decide to meditate, decide that you want to do it. It isn't complicated, but it can be challenging for some people, although that too is considered as a normal process.

Before you start meditating let me assure you that meditation won't cause you to fall in a type of trance, nor can you be brainwashed if you decide to listen to a guided meditation. This is a silly belief because these meditations are only giving you guidance for your breath, and they tell you where to send your focus. You can also find meditations with affirmations that you can listen to while you relax or sleep.

You can dedicate as little as five minutes of your day, but if you have more time, you can spend an hour in meditation.

If you are a beginner, set a shorter time such as ten to fifteen minutes, so you can get used to this process without getting frustrated.

When you start meditating: let go of any expectations about what should happen to you, what you should experience or feel during this process.

If you have expectations, you'll keep your focus on them, and you'll end up feeling irritated that you did not achieve them. This isn't a recommendation for beginners only. It happens even to people who meditate for years. For instance, I sometimes tend to expect some lovely feeling during my meditation, which is something I felt in previous meditations. When none of it happens because I am too focused on the expectations, I felt as if my meditation was not complete.

I can go on and on about what will happen to you when you calm down and start meditating, but this shouldn't be your initial point — your experience is yours only. So, relax, sit or lie down, adjust yourself, and give in to your meditation.

In the chapter where I discussed mindfulness, I wrote about how mindfulness meditation goes, and that you need to relax and let go of your thoughts so that you can allow your focus to stay on your breaths only.

There is no magical solution on how to train your focus to stay in one place. When you begin to do this, but even after, when you meditate for a long time, your focus will tend to wander.

This is a natural and normal thing, but you don't need to worry because you have control over it and you can always put it back to the thing you want it to be (a thought, mantra, breath).

Our stream of thoughts is constant — it is like a river that brings constant thoughts and words, often not connected nor meaningful.

The trick is to let these thoughts come and go without you dedicating your focus on them. Welcome that thought about your day at work, but don't stick your attention on it. Allow it to leave your mind as your main interest remains on the thing you decided to focus.

When you meditate, please make sure your main focus isn't on how to still your mind and end your stream of thoughts. This isn't possible, because you are alive. What *is* possible is to be aware of your thoughts. You are noticing them, you acknowledge them, but are strong enough not to give in and let your mind wander. But, even if that happens, you have enough power to return your focus from the sea of thoughts.

Meditation tends to awaken many parts of your memory (your subconscious), so don't be surprised to recall things you thought were long forgotten. This can be a real blessing, they come up for healing. This way I can see that my brain is a fortune chest and that even though my conscious isn't bothering me with such memories, I know that my unconscious works precisely and has stored them in files.

CHAPTER 6 – MEDITATION

How Do You Start Meditating?

Every meditation begins with the comfortable adjustment of your body. Then the conscious breathing begins. Deep breaths are your friend because they cleanse your body from stale energy. Breathing relaxes your clenching muscles and helps you relax to a point where you might want to fall asleep.

I avoid visualizing things while I am focused on my breath. My breathing is the most important thing for me at that moment, and so I leave the visualizations (if I practice such meditation) for later.

Inhale through your nose, and exhale through your mouth — although you can exhale through your nose if that feels more comfortable. Make sure you slowly fill your lungs with air and then slowly empty them. Use the breath as your massager — let it gently rub your diaphragm, lungs, and your stomach. Deep breathing will relax your body and can help you clear your physical ailments.

As you relax with the breathing, you might start seeing colours, light, but as I said earlier if you relax into it and expect nothing, then great things happen.

Brain Waves

Our brains are always in action, no matter the time of the day and if we are active or asleep. However, there is a difference between the waves that occur when you are busy and when you meditate or relax.

When you meditate, your brain creates theta waves, mostly in the middle and frontal parts. Theta waves are created when your brain is relaxed and focused on the mind activity.

Naturally, you can't measure this if you don't do an EEG, but it is scientifically proven that meditation causes the brain to produce a lot of theta waves. These waves are perfect for boosting your learning, focus, intuition, and memory, and they can only happen when you withdraw your attention from the external world.

Alpha waves, on the other hand, occur in the rear part of the brain and they too occur in abundance when you meditate (far more than when you are only relaxing). To allow your brain to create these waves you need to meditate, but if you wonder why alpha waves are important, the answer is because your brain needs them so it can relax from doing tasks such as accomplishing goals.

Delta waves occur when you sleep, but they can also appear when you are relaxing or practising meditation. Beta waves are produced when you work on your goals, such as planning or organizing a workday, but they are not nearly as abundant when you meditate.

However, when your brain relaxes by creating these brain waves, it does not mean that your mind empties. Your mind still has thoughts, although it is in a pleasant and laidback state.

Meditation is an inside job. You don't need any external sensor to relax. When your brain is relaxing from its thoughts, goals, images it saw during your active state, it uses its own power from inside.

Yes, we are that powerful.

During meditation, when your brain releases the relaxation waves is the time when you become suddenly aware that your mind tends to wander. While you meditate, you understand that you are an observer. You can call your focus back whenever you want to. Mediation can help you be aware even when you are active and notice how your thoughts are becoming negative, or your inner critic becomes loud.

CHAPTER 7

Meditation for Confidence, Acceptance, and Change of Core Beliefs

T hank you for taking the time for meditation. I hope you feel ready and relaxed to begin this process that won't take a lot of time.

This meditation is about improving your confidence, self-acceptance, and breaking old beliefs.

Before we start, please make sure your meditation time will be during the hours when you know no one will disturb you. Now is the right time to turn off the sound on your phone and pick your place.

You can sit or lie down. If you can, put on comfortable clothes. If you are laying down, take a light blanket with you if the weather isn't too hot, so you can cover yourself and feel completely relaxed.

Let's start with a few deep breaths.

Slowly inhale as much as you feel comfortable. If it is easier for you, inhale to the count of five.

Hold the breath for two seconds and then slowly exhale to the count of five.

RADIATE CONFIDENCE — Sharon Ledwith

Feel how fresh air passes through your nostrils. Feel it filling your lungs and making your stomach rise. Pay attention to the sensation it leaves when you exhale.

This is your time. You don't have to be anywhere. Relax and take another deep breath. Inhale deeply, and then slowly release the air.

Your body responds to these deep conscious breaths. It relaxes and feels a bit heavier, just like before you fall asleep.

Take another deep breath, hold it for a couple of seconds, and then let it go.

Your mind will create thoughts of all kinds, but you don't have to accept them. Welcome them, thank them for their presence, and let them dissolve.

Focus on your breath. Breathe in again, and slowly exhale. The sound of your breathing is the only thing you hear. The movements of your body as you inhale and exhale are the only things you feel right now.

There is nothing to worry about. You are safe.

Notice where your body feels tense. Is it your core? Perhaps your shoulders or neck? Imagine how your deep breath goes straight to this tensed place. Allow this healing breath to relax this part of your body.

Inhale a few more deep breaths.

Now it is time to slow down and continue breathing like you usually do.

Allow your mind to serve you a memory, any memory of a time when you were exceptionally proud of yourself.

Perhaps it was a time when you achieved a goal that you set. Maybe it was when you got a good grade, or when you graduated. Maybe it was when you got a good job.

Recall this memory and allow yourself to feel these emotions again.

You felt good and important. Your confidence was on a high level, and you felt as if though you could achieve anything.

CHAPTER 7 – MEDITATION FOR CONFIDENCE, ACCEPTANCE, AND CHANGE OF CORE BELIEFS

Allow this memory to be as vivid as possible. Remember the way you walked, talked, and acted towards people.

It feels good to be confident and to accept who you are.

Now, remember the times when you did not feel so great. Perhaps life served challenges, and you began to believe that you were not doing things so well anymore.

Remember any situation where you felt like you were not good enough, smart enough, or simply like you were doing things wrong.

Return your focus to your breath now. Slowly inhale and exhale. Let these memories dissolve as you breathe.

Reminiscing about times when you felt great and not so great is essential so you can remind yourself that everything is temporary. Not every time you feel bad means that you'll feel this way forever.

This meditation is for your benefit, to help you understand that you need to accept yourself with all your good and bad traits.

Now, visualize yourself walking on a beautiful beach. The sea is turquoise, and the sand is white, warm, and pleasant under your feet. There are palm trees, and the breeze is light.

Feel the sunshine on your skin. It feels pleasant and warm. The breeze cools you. Feel how it passes through your hair.

The scenery is magical. Everything is perfect, and you genuinely love being here.

But, when you try to take a step, you feel a massive burden stopping you from going forward. You notice there are huge chains wrapped around your waist. The chains are dragging a colossal anchor that is already sinking into the wet sand.

You do your best to take another step, and you manage to move the chains and the anchor, but somehow it feels like mission impossible to make more than a few hard steps.

You feel like crying and screaming, and when you do that, nobody is listening. You notice some people in the distance, but they don't seem like they can see you having difficulties.

You scream and wave your hands, but people don't react.

At that moment, you look down towards your waist, and you see that you only need to unhook one chain so you can release the burden.

You do that, and the chains drop. Nothing weighs you anymore. You see how the strings and the anchor sink deep into the sand and the waves cover them as if they were never there.

It was that easy. You felt this burden for a long time, and you were struggling to walk and enjoy your time and this beach, without even knowing that you were able to remove them from your body.

Now you feel light as a feather. You feel like you could fly high. You feel like running and jumping, and you start doing that.

You yell and laugh, and run and jump around the beach. This moment is your holiday. You feel so free and liberated that you feel like you could kiss and hug every person you see. You feel like hugging yourself, and you feel so happy.

You lightly walk forward towards the people, and they welcome you to join them at the beach seating.

Just like this metaphor with the beach, you can easily remove all the burden that comes with your core beliefs.

Nobody will be able to help you unhook the chain and let it drop off if you don't look into yourself and see that you are the one who needs to do that.

The chain isn't of any use for you. It does not matter why you put it on yourself, or when. It is only essential that you are now aware that it stops you from walking, running, and jumping high. When you are aware that your inability to change your core beliefs and accept yourself is only dragging you down in the wet sand, you become free. You are free to leave it all behind, and continue, light and eager, to enjoy your life.

Accept yourself for who you are — accept the way you look, the way you talk, make decisions, walk, eat. What you should change is your attitude towards the thoughts that go through your head. Notice

CHAPTER 7 – MEDITATION FOR CONFIDENCE, ACCEPTANCE, AND CHANGE OF CORE BELIEFS

them, acknowledge them, and if they serve you well, allow them to stay. If they don't serve you, say farewell, and continue with good thoughts.

Now, slowly return your focus to your breath and start breathing deeply again.

This meditation is over.

Congratulations, you did it!

You managed to breathe deeply, visualize, and observe the thoughts as they were coming and going.

Slowly move your feet, toes, hands, and shoulders. When you are ready, open your eyes. If you are starting your day now, have a pleasant and fruitful day. If you are going to sleep, rest well!

CHAPTER 8

Affirmations

Meditations and affirmations are best friends so I am dedicating a chapter with statements that will help you change your limiting beliefs.

Affirmations are one of my favourite methods whenever I notice my mind trying to convince me about something that does not serve me.

When you practice mindfulness, no matter how long it is, I recommend you recall affirmations, whichever works for you the best. During your mindful moments, you are aware of your thoughts, and I believe this is the best time to instill beliefs or healthy statements that will stay with you for a long time.

You can remember and use any of my suggestions, find audio with affirmations, or create your own. Some people like to record themselves reading their favourite affirmations because they find it more genuine listening to their voice reading these positive statements.

These are my suggestions:

Life is rewarding.

Life is fun.

Life goes easy for me.

I get great opportunities every day.

There is no such thing as a problem, only a challenge.

Challenges are great. They awaken my creativity.

I am now seeing problems as opportunities.

Things are always working out for me.

I love my life.

I choose to love everything about me.

I used to spend a lot of time complaining, but I now choose to speak great about myself and my achievements.

I appreciate my life.

I appreciate everything I have.

I appreciate the people in my life.

I appreciate that I have bills. It means I can afford to pay them.

I am now capable of seeing the fear in the eye. I am courageous.

Nothing can stop me once I set my mind on a goal.

Everything is possible for me.

The universe has my back.

I live and witness abundance every day.

I love abundance.

I love that I can afford whatever I please.

I see a thing, and I know I can afford it.

For every amount I spend, I earn three times more.

Money is energy.

I love how comfortable I feel when I have money.

Abundance and all great things come easily into my life.

I especially love when I get money from unexpected sources.

I now welcome and allow more cash flow into my life.

CHAPTER 8 – AFFIRMATIONS

Every day I am doing something that my future self will be grateful for.

I am now capable of seeing my limiting beliefs and knowing that they are not real.

My limiting beliefs are slowly dissolving like salt in water.

I know that I am worthy of love.

I see myself in the mirror, and I smile to myself because I know that things are going well for me.

I now choose to see only the best in me, both physically and mentally.

It is easy for me to notice a thought that does not serve me and let it go.

It is easy for me to switch to positive thinking.

It is easy for me to accept myself in every meaning of the word.

I am worthy.

I am enough.

I am loveable.

It is easy for me to meet people that appreciate me.

It is easy for me to dedicate my attention to my goals.

I achieve my goals with gratitude.

I am optimistic.

I am grateful for every downfall I had because I now know that it was only a lesson for my greater good.

I accept myself just the way I am.

I am no longer in a race with people. I don't compete with anyone.

There is no need for me to compare myself to anyone. Everyone has a different life, views, thoughts, and opportunities.

I love who I am becoming.

I love how my body looks.

I love how my vibration slowly rises.

I love how I successfully change my core beliefs.

I now forgive people who hurt me, because I know they were hurt too and did not understand better.

I forgive myself for every choice I did that did not flatter me.

I forgive myself for staying in certain moods for a long time. I am grateful that I went that road so now I know I am capable of loving and accepting myself.

I forgive my parents for raising me the way they did. They were doing the best they could.

My respect for myself grows stronger every day.

Other people respect me for who I am.

My relationship with myself is healthy.

My respect and love for myself set the conditions for others to love me and respect me.

Other people love me.

My ideas are heard and respected.

My work is valued and respected.

I now know that I can achieve anything.

I am determined and don't give up on my goals and dreams.

I work on boosting my confidence because I love being confident.

Being confident suits me.

My confidence does not depend on others.

I can speak with confidence naturally.

I can easily say no when I don't feel like doing something.

I can easily stand up for myself.

CHAPTER 8 – AFFIRMATIONS

I upgrade my knowledge every day.

I want to learn things that help me grow as a person.

Every day my confidence is stronger.

I deserve to change myself for the better.

I enjoy feeling happy, content, and at peace.

I am grateful for my peaceful thoughts.

I appreciate my ability to guide my thoughts in the right direction.

I am free to choose, and now I want to feel good.

I let go of my former habit to criticize myself.

My mind is clearer every day.

Meditation helps me to become aware of my thoughts.

I am mindful.

Every day I learn to challenge myself out of the comfort zone without feeling fear.

I am no longer scared of mistakes as I know that they are a normal thing.

I am truly and honestly happy.

I end every day with gratitude for the things and people in my life.

I start every day with gratitude for my will and need to improve my beliefs.

My focus goes only on things, people, and situations that make me feel good.

I now know that I am worthy of happiness.

I choose happiness because it brings the best in me and boosts my confidence.

I live in the present moment without burdening myself with thoughts of the past or future.

Conclusion

The importance of working on your confidence is for your personal emotional and physical benefits. You're not working on your confidence so other people will say, "Oh, look at him/her; they are so confident and do things so well."

Your primary goal is to boost your confidence so you'll feel good about who you are, as well as your goals, choices, decisions, and the way you dress and speak, and interact with others.

You are confident.

Awaken your positive inner feelings and shut down that loud inner critic that wants to make you believe in things that are not real. To improve your self-image, and the way you feel about yourself, make a decision that you want to do it. This decision and need to feel better must be stronger than your need to find flaws in yourself and your experiences.

Building your confidence doesn't happen overnight, but don't let this set you back as the process is far better than the result. You shouldn't worry or be obsessed with the final result, because as long as you are alive, you can work on yourself and self-improvement.

I often tell people that they need to take their childhood years as a base that will help them move forward in building their confidence. Young children are not burdened with what other kids think of them, what they wear, how they play games and so on. Children only care about having a good time and playing with friends.

Think of those years as your initial point. Going back to your childhood isn't possible, but you can inspire yourself to nurture your inner child and boost the confidence you were not even aware you had before life happened to you.

Challenge yourself to become a person who is aware of all the great things you do. When you are aware of yourself and the moment you live in, it's easy to be happy with little things and do what you want to do because you know it will make you feel better.

To allow your confidence to shine again, accept that your most significant enemy and the only person who stands in your way is you. We often believe that others are doing bad things to us, but nobody can hurt us worse than ourselves.

Through the years, we have all collected beliefs from others, including parents, grandparents, teachers, friends, TV, films, and shows without being aware we believed in these things. We put our focus on these beliefs and decided to shut our eyes to anything else.

You can prove to yourself that you can earn money even if you don't work super hard, but your beliefs that "money doesn't grow on trees" or that "earning money isn't easy" are so deeply embedded in your mind, that you don't see that those statements are not real.

To change the way you see yourself and how you live your life, you'll have to change your old beliefs.

Core beliefs can make us believe that life is hard, that we are not good enough, that we are not lovable, smart, or skilled. To change these beliefs, become more mindful about the present moment. Become aware of the moment you are in, without allowing your mind to think and plan what you'll do in the next moment, in a day, a week or two months from now.

Many of us tend to live in a future moment and don't pay attention to the present moment. We let anxiety take control over by thinking and planning for the future, and then we wonder why we feel bad.

To be present at the moment, you have to learn to still your mind and let it focus on right now. Mindfulness isn't a tricky thing, and everybody is capable of doing it. To start, I suggest you practice mindfulness meditations as when you are mindful; you can notice how your mind is producing thousands of unconnected thoughts that don't serve you.

When you're aware, you can detect negative self-talk, the inner critic, and thoughts that are bad for you. A mindful person will notice such thoughts and will shift their focus to something more beneficial.

As you learn to be mindful, you learn how to recognize that your thoughts are the main reason why you have emotions. A thought

CONCLUSION

you return to over and over again can bear negative or pleasant feelings — it is up to you as to which. When you worry about the future and overthink, you will feel bad, depressed, sad, and anxious.

When you reminiscence about the past and wonder how things could have gone if you had only made a different decision, you're missing out on the present moment, and such a habit will only bring sadness.

Our old beliefs can keep us safe in the comfort zone, but being safe does not mean that you'll be happy. Changing your core beliefs means that you'll be able to make new decisions and come out of the comfort zone.

I spent years working a job that I truly disliked when I wanted to spend more time with my children and do something that pleased me. I was not able to see my talents until I set a goal to read and educate myself on spirituality. It was not until I decided to work on my spirituality and teach myself that I was able to quit my old job and start doing what I truly wanted to do for a living.

Setting goals can work miracles for your confidence. When you realize you are capable of achieving and succeeding, you feel like nothing can stop you. When you know that you can do anything you want, this is when the shift happens. You accept yourself, a method that will help you become a better version of yourself.

We live in a world where we are always told that if we do this or that, look a certain way, wear a specific piece of clothing, we will be accepted. The results are millions of people who feel like they don't belong anywhere — people who feel unsatisfied, discontent, and have suffocated their confidence.

To accept yourself means to be entirely open with yourself. Do you like the places you go? Do you feel comfortable wearing the clothes you wear? Do you feel like the choices you make are honest, or do you make them to impress others?

When you learn to accept yourself and all your virtues and flaws, and all the things you like and dislike, you can hold your head high and walk proudly because you'll be free from society's burdens.

We've discussed the many methods that can help you notice all the good things about yourself and become aware of all the blessings you have. Keep a journal of your achievements. When you forget about the things you did successfully, open your journal, and remind yourself. Be grateful for everything that you have starting from your health to the smallest things, such as waking up and breathing.

Be thankful for the people in your life, even the ones who may have made you feel bad. Thank the universe or God for these people because they were all teaching you a lesson either by loving you and helping you or by causing you to see what you didn't want in your life.

Meditate whenever you can as it will change your life for the better. Dedicate ten to fifteen minutes a day to meditate to calm your mind. Learn where your focus goes and how you can quickly shift when negative thoughts occur. Let your brain create brain waves that are regenerative and beneficial for you.

Read as much as possible. Enrich your knowledge for things in which you have an interest. If your focus is on becoming a better version of yourself, manifesting your wishes, achieving your goals, and changing your beliefs, start reading books related to these things as you are doing now.

Learn more about the law of attraction and how we all vibrate all the time. Vibration is the key to the universe. We get a response from the universe, the creator, God, or life, whatever you want to call it, all the time — it just changes depending upon our vibration.

When your vibration is lower, and your focus is on the negative things, you end up getting more of the negative things. If you focus on the things you don't want, the universe serves you more of what you don't want. This is why it's essential to learn how to shift your focus and change your thoughts. Remember, your mind is your biggest weapon. The more you train it through meditations, mindfulness, visualizations, and switching to positive thoughts, the more you'll witness the greatness of life and achieve the things you want to have.

But, you can wish, work, visualize, meditate, and have a positive mind, but if you are not ready to receive, nor are you allowing the

CONCLUSION

things you want to manifest, then you won't witness the changes. It is essential to believe that you'll get them.

I wanted a change. I wanted to work at what I do today, so I set a goal and made it happen. I was excited about creating a new career, without burdening myself about the date or the outcome. I felt joyful to see my manifestations, and I was open to receiving. This is how I became who I am today. I visualized myself helping people, talking, and guiding them to overcome their blocks. It took me less than one year to leave my old job once I started the process. Meanwhile, I worked on my education and started my business. Today I have a holistic clinic called Healing Touch located in Athenry Co. Galway in Ireland.

I help people heal their thoughts and improve their lives. With my help, they work on clearing the blocks that are stopping them from seeing their worth, potential, and from boosting their confidence. Today I am a spiritual therapist, and I guide people to achieve success and believe in themselves.

I created an online course of eight weeks (Empower Yourself and Radiate confidence), where I help people create more changes and improve their lives. And, now, an author. I manifested all of this within three years. If I can achieve this, then absolutely you can too!

Your mindset is everything. You may have doubts, feel like things might not work out, but at least give it a try. See this as a work and investment in yourself, and allow yourself to be surprised with the outcome. The only thing you'll lose is the old beliefs that are holding you back, your self-doubts, and your inability to see your potential.

You indeed are capable of radiating confidence. Awaken it today!!!

You can check all of the info on my website:

www.healingtouchbysl.com

Here, you'll find my guided meditations, online courses, and can book an appointment with me.

Also, you can seek me out on Facebook (Healing Touch Athenry).

Printed in Poland
by Amazon Fulfillment
Poland Sp. z o.o., Wrocław